ALL-TIME-FAVORITE RECIPES
From

SOUTH CAROLINA

COOKS

Dedication

For every cook who wants to create amazing
recipes from the great state of South Carolina.

Appreciation

Thanks to all our South Carolina cooks who shared
their delightful and delicious recipes with us!

Gooseberry Patch
An imprint of Globe Pequot
64 South Main Street
Essex, CT 06426
www.gooseberrypatch.com
1 800 854 6673

Copyright 2024, Gooseberry Patch
978-162093-559-0

Do you have a tried & true recipe...tip, craft or
memory that you'd like to see featured in a
Gooseberry Patch cookbook? Visit our website at
www.gooseberrypatch.com and follow the easy steps
to submit your favorite family recipe.

Or send them to us at:

Gooseberry Patch
PO Box 812
Columbus, OH 43216-0812

Don't forget to include the number of servings your
recipe makes, plus your name, address, phone
number and email address. If we select your recipe,
your name will appear right along with it...and you'll
receive a FREE copy of the book!

SOUTH CAROLINA
ICONIC SOUTH CAROLINA

Breathtaking views of cloud-kissed mountains, rich forests and miles of sun-painted beaches are the amazing land formations that throughout history have blended together, birthing a rich and diverse culture with a strong sense of community and neighborliness throughout the great state of South Carolina.

Settled by Native Americans over 50,000 years ago and joined by English settlers in the 1600s, South Carolina became a place where amazing historical events and delicious cuisines that have stood the test of time, were created!

South Carolina is one of the few places where you might come across a 500-year-old tree and an island full of monkeys all while on the hunt for a hole-in-one at one of the 300 putt-putt courses that are available.

Under the shade of a palmetto tree, it is common to find meals shared outdoors with family, neighbors and friends. Traditionally, these gatherings often include dishes like Frogmore Stew, barbecue, oysters, shrimp & grits, boiled peanuts, pimento cheese and fresh peaches.

Inside this cookbook you will find delicious tried & true recipes from cooks all around the great state of South Carolina, including Dee's Carolina Seafood Chowder, Dressed Oyster Po'Boys, The Bay's Pepper Slaw, Saucy Ribs, Slow-Cooker Balsamic Chicken, South-of-the-Boarder Breakfast, Savory Low-Country Shrimp & Cheese Grits and Mattie Lou's Prune Cake. Enjoy!

OUR STORY

Back in 1984, our families were neighbors in little Delaware, Ohio. With small children, we wanted to do what we loved and stay home with the kids too. We had always shared a love of home cooking and so, **Gooseberry Patch** was born.

Almost immediately, we found a connection with our customers and it wasn't long before these friends started sharing recipes. Since then we've enjoyed publishing hundreds of cookbooks with your tried & true recipes.

We know we couldn't have done it without our friends all across the country and we look forward to continuing to build a community with you. Welcome to the **Gooseberry Patch** family!

JoAnn & Vickie

TABLE OF CONTENTS

CHAPTER ONE

BLUE RIDGE
Breakfasts

ENJOY THESE TASTY BREAKFAST
RECIPES THAT BRING YOU TO THE
TABLE WITH A HEARTY "GOOD
MORNING!" AND CARRY YOU
THROUGH THE DAY TO TACKLE
WHATEVER COMES YOUR WAY.

APPLE JACK MUFFINS

**ZOE BENNETT
COLUMBIA, SC**

The best combination...apples and cinnamon.

2-1/3 c. all-purpose flour
1 c. plus
3 T. sugar, divided
1 T. baking powder
4 t. cinnamon, divided
1 t. baking soda
1/2 t. salt
1-1/2 c. apples, peeled,
   cored and finely
   chopped
1 c. buttermilk
1/3 c. milk
1/3 c. ricotta cheese
3 T. oil
1 T. vanilla extract
2 egg whites
1 egg, beaten

In a large bowl, sift together flour, one cup sugar, baking powder, 2 teaspoons cinnamon, baking soda and salt. Fold in apples; stir, then make a well in the center. Whisk together remaining ingredients; pour into well in flour mixture. Gently stir until just moistened. Spoon batter equally into 18 greased muffin cups. Combine remaining sugar and cinnamon; sprinkle evenly over batter. Bake at 400 degrees for 18 minutes, or until a toothpick inserted in a muffin tests clean.

Makes 1-1/2 dozen.

KITCHEN TIP

Making homemade whipped cream is simple. The key is to use a metal bowl that has been refrigerated for at least 10 minutes prior to whipping your cream.

SPINACH QUICHE

GLORIA TOLBERT
MOORE, SC

This is my go-to recipe for brunches and get-togethers. No matter where I bring it, everyone always asks me for the recipe!

In a bowl, mix together all ingredients except crust; pour into crust. Bake at 400 degrees for 30 to 45 minutes, until golden and center is set. Cut into wedges.

Serves 6.

12-oz. pkg. frozen spinach soufflé, thawed

2 eggs, beaten

3 T. milk

2 t. onion, chopped

3/4 c. Italian ground pork sausage, browned and drained

1/2 c. sliced mushrooms

3/4 c. shredded Swiss cheese

9-inch pie crust, baked

CREAMY EGG BAKE

DEBRA JOHNSON
MYRTLE BEACH, SC

Everyone gets their own little breakfast portion...just add some hot buttered toast!

2 t. butter, softened

3 T. whipping cream

8 eggs

salt and pepper to taste

4 t. fresh chives, minced

4 t. grated Parmesan cheese

Spread butter inside 4 ramekins or custard cups. Divide cream evenly among ramekins. Crack 2 eggs into each ramekin, keeping yolks unbroken. Season with salt and pepper; sprinkle with chives and cheese. Set ramekins on a baking sheet. Bake at 325 degrees for 12 to 15 minutes, until egg whites have set and yolks are still soft. Remove from oven. Let stand for a few minutes before serving.

Makes 4 servings.

SWISS & CHEDDAR BAKED GRITS

ZOE BENNETT
COLUMBIA, SC

Down south, it just wouldn't be breakfast without creamy grits on the menu! For an extra special brunch, top portions with sautéed shrimp.

In a heavy saucepan over medium heat, bring water and 1/2 teaspoon salt to a boil. Gradually stir in grits; return to a boil. Cover and reduce heat to medium-low. Simmer, stirring occasionally, for 5 minutes, or until grits are set. Remove from heat. Stir in butter, remaining salt, pepper and 1-1/4 cups Cheddar cheese. Let stand for 15 minutes; stir in eggs. Pour half of grits mixture into a lightly greased 12"x8" baking pan. Sprinkle Swiss cheese over top. Spoon remaining grits mixture over cheese. Cover and bake at 350 degrees for one hour, or until set. Uncover; sprinkle remaining Cheddar cheese over top. Bake, uncovered, for 5 minutes, or until cheese melts.

Makes 8 to 10 servings.

4-1/2 c. water
3/4 t. salt, divided
1-1/4 c. quick-cooking grits, uncooked
1/4 c. butter
1-1/2 c. shredded Cheddar cheese, divided
1/4 t. pepper
3 eggs, beaten
1-1/1 c. shredded Swiss cheese

JUST FOR FUN

There are no major professional sports teams in South Carolina. That's right, no NFL, NHL, NBA, MLS or MLB. However, Myrtle Beach is the Golf Capital of the world, and South Carolina has more than 300 public and private golf courses in total.

FRUIT & OAT BARS

**LESLIE HARVIE
SIMPSONVILLE, SC**

*When I was a child, my mother would whip up a batch of these yummy
bars every Saturday morning. Strawberry was my favorite flavor!*

15-1/4 oz. pkg. yellow
  cake mix
2-1/2 c. quick-cooking
  oats, uncooked
3/4 c. butter, melted
12-oz. jar favorite-flavor
  jam or preserves
1 T. water

In a large bowl, combine dry cake mix and oats.
Add melted butter; mix until crumbly. Add half of
crumb mixture to a greased 13"x9" baking pan;
press firmly to cover bottom of pan. Stir together
jam or preserves and water; spoon over layer in
pan. Cover with remaining crumb mixture. Pat firmly
to form an even layer. Bake at 375 degrees for 20
minutes. Cool and cut into bars.

Makes 1-1/2 dozen.

SWEET & SPICY BACON

**KAREN SMITH
ROCK HILL, SC**

Try this easy-to-fix bacon at your next brunch...guests will love it!

1/2 c. brown sugar,
  packed
2 T. chili powder
1 t. ground cumin
1 t. cumin seed
1 t. ground coriander
1/4 t. cayenne pepper
10 thick slices bacon

Line a 15"x10" jelly-roll pan with aluminum foil.
Place a wire rack on pan and set aside. Combine all
ingredients except bacon; sprinkle mixture onto a
large piece of wax paper. Press bacon into mixture,
turning to coat well. Arrange in a single layer on
prepared pan; place pan on center rack of oven.
Bake at 400 degrees for 12 minutes; turn bacon
over. Bake for an additional 10 minutes, until deep
golden. Drain on paper towels; serve warm.

Serves 4 to 5.

ABUELA'S GARLIC GRITS

**KELLY PETTY
AIKEN, SC**

*My grandmother's most-requested recipe. Her name was Frances, but my
daughter lovingly called her Abuela (Spanish for grandmother) because she
was a Spanish professor.*

In a saucepan over high heat, bring water and salt
to a boil. Slowly stir in grits; cook 3 to 5 minutes,
stirring constantly. Remove from heat. Add butter
and cheese, stirring until melted. Beat eggs, milk and
garlic powder together; stir into hot mixture. Pour
into an ungreased 13"x9" glass baking pan. Sprinkle
with cereal and hot sauce. Bake, uncovered, at 350
degrees for one hour. Let stand 15 minutes before
serving.

Serves 10 to 12.

4-1/2 c. water

1 t. salt

1 c. quick-cooking grits,
uncooked

1/2 c. butter, cubed

3/4 lb. pasteurized
process cheese spread,
cubed

2 eggs, beaten

2/3 c. milk

1/4 t. garlic powder

1 c. wheat & barley
cereal nuggets

hot pepper sauce to
taste

JUST FOR FUN

Morgan Island (Monkey Island), a barrier
island on South Carolina's eastern seashore,
is home to over 4,000 rhesus monkeys and no
permanent human inhabitants. The species were
brought over for scientific research and found
a permanent home on an island without many
predators. It is now the only place in the United
States where so many monkeys roam freely.

SAVORY LOW-COUNTRY SHRIMP & CHEESE GRITS

**SHARON CANDLER
CHARLESTON, SC**

Serve this classic low-country favorite with some warm, crusty bread and a fresh spinach salad.

6 c. chicken broth
3/4 t. salt
1-1/2 c. long-cooking grits, uncooked
1 green pepper, chopped
1/2 red pepper, chopped
6 green onions, chopped
2 cloves garlic, minced
1-1/2 lb. uncooked small shrimp, peeled
2 T. butter
1-1/2 c. shredded sharp Cheddar cheese
1-1/2 c. shredded Monterey Jack cheese
2 10-oz. cans diced tomatoes with green chiles, drained
1/4 t. cayenne pepper, or to taste

Combine broth, salt and grits in a slow cooker; stir well. Cover and cook on low setting for 8 hours. About 2 hours before serving, in a skillet over medium heat, sauté peppers, onions, garlic and shrimp in butter until shrimp turn pink. Add pepper mixture to slow cooker along with cheeses, tomatoes and cayenne pepper. Stir well. Cover and cook on high setting for 2 hours longer.

Serves 6 to 8.

HAM & CHEESE BREAKFAST BITES

**PAIGE BEAR
LYMAN, SC**

*This is a quick breakfast that's easily made ahead of time and reheated.
I keep a bag of these in my fridge for my husband to eat.*

In a large bowl, whisk together eggs, milk, baking mix and seasonings. Add ham, onions, tomato, cheese and 2 tablespoons salsa; mix well. Spoon egg mixture into 12 muffin cups sprayed with non-stick vegetable spray, filling almost full. Bake at 350 degrees for 35 minutes. Let stand in pan for another 5 minutes. Serve warm with remaining salsa.

Makes one dozen.

4 eggs, beaten
1/2 c. milk or almond milk
1/4 c. biscuit baking mix
1/2 t. dried oregano
1/4 t. kosher salt
1/4 t. pepper
3/4 c. cooked ham, diced
2 green onions, chopped
1 tomato, chopped
3 T. shredded Cheddar cheese
1/2 c. favorite salsa, divided

MOM'S SWEET APPLE OMELET

**KRISTY MARKNERS
FORT MILL, SC**

*This is a recipe my mom has been making as long as I can remember.
My brother and I used to fight over who could eat the last serving...it's
that good!*

Whisk together all ingredients. Pour into an ungreased 9" pie plate. Bake, uncovered, at 350 degrees for one hour, or until center is firm. Cut into wedges; serve warm.

Makes 8 servings.

4 c. applesauce
1 c. sugar
3 eggs, beaten
1 T. cinnamon

HAM & CORN GRIDDLE CAKES

ZOE BENNETT
COLUMBIA, SC

I had some leftover ham and corn from the previous night's dinner, so I thought I might try using them up for breakfast the next day. With a little creativity and trial & error, I came up with these scrumptious griddle cakes.

1-1/3 c. all-purpose
  flour
1/2 c. yellow cornmeal
1 T. baking powder
2 T. sugar
2 t. salt
2 eggs, beaten
1/2 c. milk
2 T. oil
15-oz. can creamed
  corn
1 c. corn
1 c. cooked ham, finely
  diced
oil for frying
Garnish: cinnamon
  applesauce
Optional: powdered
  sugar

In a large bowl, stir together flour, cornmeal, baking powder, sugar and salt. In a separate bowl, combine eggs, milk, oil and creamed corn. Add egg mixture to flour mixture; stir well. Fold in corn and ham. Heat 1/2 inch oil in a large skillet over medium heat. For each griddle cake, ladle 1/2 cup of batter into hot oil. Cook until edges are dry and bottom is golden. Flip and cook other side until golden. Serve griddlecakes with warm applesauce and a dusting of powdered sugar, if desired.

Serves 3 to 6.

FARMHOUSE BREAKFAST BAKE

**KAREN SMITH
ROCK HILL, SC**

Wedges of this hearty farm-style breakfast are terrific served with a frosty glass of orange juice.

Place pie crust in a 9" pie plate on a baking sheet; sprinkle sausage in crust. Top with potatoes, onion, red or green pepper and 1/4 cup cheese; set aside. Beat together eggs, milk, seasoned salt and pepper; pour over sausage mixture in crust. Bake for 30 minutes at 375 degrees, or until egg mixture is set and crust is lightly golden. Sprinkle with remaining cheese.

Serves 6.

9-inch pie crust, unbaked

1/2 lb. ground pork sausage, browned and drained

1 c. frozen diced potatoes, thawed

1/4 c. green onion, sliced

1/4 c. red or green pepper, chopped

1/2 c. shredded sharp Cheddar cheese, divided

4 eggs

1/4 c. milk

1/4 t. seasoned salt

1/4 t. pepper

DINNERTIME CONVERSATION

Charleston was home to the first public college, the first museum and the first playhouse ever in the United States.

CRANBERRY-DATE SPREAD

NANCY KAISER
YORK, SC

This spread is great on homemade rolls and biscuits, or on toast for breakfast in the morning. I make this every Thanksgiving and Christmas.

1 c. water
1 c. sugar
12-oz. pkg. fresh cranberries, rinsed
4-oz. pkg. chopped dates
1/2 c. chopped walnuts or pecans

In a medium saucepan, combine water and sugar; stir to dissolve sugar. Bring to a boil over medium heat. Add cranberries and dates; return to a boil. Reduce heat to medium-low. Simmer gently for about 10 minutes, stirring occasionally. Remove from heat and cool; stir in nuts. Cover and refrigerate up to 2 weeks.

Makes about 3 cups.

CHEESY SOUTHERN GRITS

ZOE BENNETT
COLUMBIA, SC

At our house, it wouldn't be breakfast without grits! We love them alongside scrambled eggs and crispy bacon.

1-1/2 c. stone-ground or regular long-cooking grits, uncooked
6 c. water
1 c. whipping cream
1-1/2 to
2 T. butter, softened
1 T. salt
Optional: small amount of milk
1 c. shredded sharp Cheddar cheese

In a slow cooker, combine all ingredients except optional milk and cheese. Cover and cook on low setting for 6 to 8 hours, stirring occasionally. If mixture starts to dry out, stir in a little milk. About 15 to 30 minutes before serving time, stir in cheese; cover and finish cooking.

Makes 8 servings.

BAKED BREAKFAST GOODNESS

KRISTY MARKNERS
FORT MILL, SC

My two-year-old daughter just loves oatmeal. I got tired of fixing her the same old instant packet everyday, so I came up with this recipe. I like it just as much as she does! For a slimmed-down version, use unsweetened almond milk and powdered sweetener.

Stir together applesauce, sugar, egg white and milk in a bowl. Add cereal, baking powder and spices; stir until well combined. Fold in fruit. Spoon into an 8"x6" baking pan sprayed with non-stick vegetable spray. Bake, uncovered, at 350 degrees for 30 minutes

Makes 4 servings.

1/4 c. unsweetened applesauce

1/2 c. sugar or low-calorie powdered sweetener blend for baking

3 T. egg white substitute, beaten

1/2 c. milk or unsweetened almond milk

1-1/2 c. multi-grain hot cereal, uncooked

1 t. baking powder

1/2 t. cinnamon

1/8 t. ground ginger

1 banana, diced

1 /4 c. dried wild blueberries

SIMPLE BRUNCH QUICHE

ZOE BENNETT
COLUMBIA, SC

Make this quiche just the way you like it! Some delicious variations are Swiss cheese & crispy bacon or Monterey Jack with salsa and black olives.

1 c. shredded Cheddar
  cheese
6 eggs, beaten
1/2 c. milk
2 T. fresh chives,
  chopped
1/4 t. salt
1/8 t. pepper
1 c. water

Wrap a 7" springform pan with aluminum foil, leaving some excess for handles on each side. Spray pan with non-stick vegetable spray; spread cheese in pan and set aside. In a bowl, whisk together eggs, milk, chives and seasonings; pour over cheese in pan. Place a rack or trivet in a 5-quart electric pressure cooker; add water and set pan on rack. Close and lock lid. Select high pressure for 30 minutes, making sure the valve in the lid is closed. After 30 minutes, turn off pressure cooker and let stand 10 minutes. Open pressure cooker using quick release method. Remove pan using foil handles; let cool slightly and slice into wedges.

Makes 4 servings.

JUST FOR FUN

On Hilton Head Island is a mysterious circle of 4,000-year-old shells called the Sea Pines Shell Ring. It may have been a ceremonial area for Native Americans.

STRAWBERRY-BANANA SCONES

KRISTY MARKNERS
FORT MILL, SC

My mother-in-law and I took the kids strawberry picking, and we ended up with four gallons of strawberries! This was one of many recipes I created to use them all up.

Line an 8"x6" baking pan with aluminum foil; place unpeeled banana in pan. Bake at 350 degrees for 15 minutes. Peel banana; mash in a small bowl. In a separate bowl, combine baking mix, milk, egg, almond extract and sugar. Fold in strawberries and banana. Press dough evenly into the aluminum foil-lined baking pan. Lift out foil; cut dough into 6 equal portions. Place on a parchment-lined baking sheet. Bake at 350 degrees for 18 to 20 minutes, or until golden.

Makes 6.

1 banana
1-2/3 c. biscuit baking mix
1/4 c. milk
1 egg, beaten
1 t. almond extract
1/4 c. sugar
3/4 c. strawberries, hulled and diced

COUNTRY BREAKFAST SANDWICHES

KAREN SMITH
ROCK HILL, SC

Why not try pancakes or toasted bagels in place of the toast for a change? So scrumptious!

Heat 2 tablespoons butter in a skillet over low heat. Add apple; sauté until tender and golden, turning often. Spread toasted bread with remaining butter; top each slice with sausages, apple slices and syrup.

Makes 2 servings.

3 T. butter, divided
1 Granny Smith apple, peeled, cored and thinly sliced
2 slices whole-wheat bread, toasted
3 links pork sausage, halved lengthwise and browned
1/4 c. maple syrup, warmed

BLACKBERRY FRENCH TOAST

VALERIE GARDNER
LYMAN, SC

My sister-in-law shared this recipe with me. It's perfect if you have overnight company and don't want to spend all morning in the kitchen. Just make it up the night before, then pull it out of the fridge in the morning to bake. Voilà! You've got a yummy breakfast without much effort at all.

1 c. blackberry jam

3/4-lb. loaf French bread, cut into 1-1/2 inch cubes and divided

8-oz. pkg. cream cheese, cubed

1 to 2 c. fresh blackberries

4 eggs, beaten

2 c. half-and-half

1 t. cinnamon

1 t. vanilla extract

1/2 c. brown sugar, packed

Garnish: maple syrup, whipped cream, sliced fresh fruit

Spoon jam into a small saucepan over medium heat. Cook for one to 2 minutes until melted and smooth, stirring once; remove from heat. Spread half the bread cubes in a lightly greased 13"x9" baking pan. Top with cream cheese cubes and blackberries; drizzle with melted jam. Top with remaining bread cubes. In a large bowl, whisk together eggs, half-and-half, cinnamon and vanilla; pour over bread mixture. Sprinkle with brown sugar. Cover tightly with aluminum foil; refrigerate overnight. Bake, covered, at 325 degrees for 20 minutes. Uncover and bake 15 more minutes, or until bread is golden and mixture is set. Serve with maple syrup, garnished as desired.

Serves 8 to 10.

MINI CHEDDAR SOUFFLÉS

ZOE BENNETT
COLUMBIA, SC

Scrumptious on a holiday buffet spread.

Melt butter in a saucepan over medium heat. Stir in flour; cook and stir for one minute. Gradually add milk; stir until well blended. Cook and stir until mixture comes to a boil. Remove from heat; stir in cheese until melted. Mix in mustard and bacon. Cool slightly. Stir in egg yolks one at a time; set aside. With an electric mixer on medium speed, beat egg whites until stiff but not dry, about 5 minutes. Gently fold into cheese mixture. Spoon into 12 lightly greased non-stick muffin cups or ramekins. Bake at 350 degrees for about 25 minutes, until puffed and set. Serve warm, garnished as desired.

Makes 12.

- 3 T. butter
- 3 T. all-purpose flour
- 3/4 c. milk
- 3/4 c. shredded Cheddar cheese
- 1 T. Dijon mustard
- 4 slices bacon, crisply cooked and crumbled
- 4 eggs, separated
- Optional: fresh parsley or chives, chopped

CREAM CHEESE DANISH

ROBIN LONG
NEWBERRY, SC

Did you get out of bed on the wrong side today? You'll feel so much better after you've tasted this!

Blend together cream cheese and sugar in a large bowl; add egg yolk, lemon juice and vanilla. Set aside. Layer one tube of crescent rolls in bottom of a greased 13"x9" baking pan; press seams together. Spread cream cheese mixture over top; layer remaining tube of rolls on top of cream cheese. Bake at 350 degrees for 15 to 20 minutes, until golden. Let cool. Mix together powdered sugar and milk to a thin consistency; drizzle over top. Cut into slices to serve.

Serves 15 to 20.

- 2 8-oz. pkgs. cream cheese, softened
- 3/4 c. sugar
- 1 egg yolk, beaten
- 2 t. lemon juice
- 1 t. vanilla extract
- 2 8-oz. tubes refrigerated crescent rolls
- 2 c. powdered sugar
- 4 to 5 T. milk

CRUSTLESS BROCCOLI QUICHE

DEBRA JOHNSON
MYRTLE BEACH, SC

This is a very versatile recipe...in springtime I like to use asparagus instead of broccoli. It's a great way to use up leftover shredded cheeses you may have in the fridge.

6 eggs
2 T. all-purpose flour
1/2 t. salt
pepper to taste
1/8 t. nutmeg
1 c. half-and-half
1 c. whole milk
3 c. cooked broccoli
  or other vegetable,
  chopped and well-
  drained
2 T. fresh basil, minced
1 c. shredded Gruyère
  cheese
1 c. shredded Parmesan
  cheese, divided

In a bowl, beat eggs with flour and seasonings; whisk in half-and-half and milk. Stir in broccoli, basil, Gruyère cheese and 1/2 cup Parmesan cheese. Pour egg mixture into a well-greased large slow cooker. Sprinkle remaining Parmesan cheese on top. Cover and cook on high setting for 1-1/2 hours, or until just set in the center. To serve, run a knife around the edge of quiche; cut into wedges.

Makes 6 servings.

STUFFED BANANA FRENCH TOAST

KAREN SMITH
ROCK HILL, SC

Take just a little extra time for a breakfast that tells your family, "You're special!"

Cut a pocket in the side of each slice of bread without cutting all the way through. Stuff 6 banana slices into each pocket; set aside. Whisk together remaining ingredients in a shallow bowl. Soak bread slices in mixture, turning once. Heat a lightly greased skillet over medium-low heat. Cook bread until golden, about 2 minutes on each side. Transfer to an aluminum foil-lined 13"x9" baking pan that has been sprayed with non-stick vegetable spray; bake at 350 degrees for 8 minutes. Serve with warm Maple-Pecan Syrup.

Serves 4.

Maple-Pecan Syrup:
Combine ingredients in a small saucepan over medium heat; simmer for 5 minutes. Discard cinnamon stick.

4 thick slices country-style bread
1 banana, thinly sliced
4 eggs
1/3 c. milk
1 t. sugar
3/4 t. vanilla extract
1/8 t. nutmeg
1/8 t. salt

MAPLE-PECAN SYRUP:
1 c. maple syrup
4-inch cinnamon stick
1 T. butter
1 t. vanilla extract
1 c. pecan halves

SOUTH-OF-THE-BORDER BREAKFAST

DEBRA JOHNSON
MYRTLE BEACH, SC

We love to serve this hearty, spicy dish when having special friends over for brunch.

10 eggs
1 t. dried thyme
salt and pepper to taste
7-1/2 oz. pkg. corn tortillas
8-oz. pkg. shredded Cheddar cheese, divided
10-oz. can Mexican-style diced tomatoes with green chiles, divided
1 lb. ground mild pork sausage, browned and drained
4-oz. can chopped green chiles
Optional: chopped jalapeños to taste, tortilla chips, sour cream, guacamole

Beat eggs with thyme, salt and pepper; set aside. Layer tortillas, one cup cheese, half the tomatoes, sausage, chiles, jalapeños if using, egg mixture, remaining cheese and tomatoes in a greased 2-quart casserole dish. Bake at 350 degrees for 30 minutes, until eggs are set. Top with crushed tortilla chips, sour cream and guacamole, if desired.

Serves 4 to 6.

KITCHEN TIP

Main dishes that can be refrigerated overnight are great stress-free menu choices when serving breakfast or brunch.

CORNMEAL BUTTERMILK WAFFLES

ZOE BENNETT
COLUMBIA, SC

These old-fashioned waffles are delicious! Mom gave me the recipe from a booklet she got back in the 1970s. Serve with butter and maple syrup, or topped with creamed chicken for brunch.

In a saucepan over medium heat, bring water to a boil. Add cornmeal, stirring until smooth. Stir in butter until melted; remove from heat and let stand until slightly cooled. Beat in egg yolks; add buttermilk. Beat well and set aside. In a bowl, combine flour, baking powder, baking soda, sugar and salt. Add cornmeal mixture, stir just until moistened. In another bowl, beat egg whites to stiff peaks with an electric mixer on high speed. Gently fold egg whites into batter, stirring just until blended. Pour 1/2 cup batter per waffle into a preheated, greased waffle iron. Bake according to manufacturer's directions.

Makes 4 waffles.

1-1/2 c. water
1/2 c. yellow cornmeal
3 T. butter
3 eggs, separated
3/4 c. buttermilk
1 c. all-purpose flour
2 t. baking powder
1/2 t. baking soda
1 T. sugar
1/2 t. salt

CHAPTER TWO

SHORELINE

Salads & Sides

TOSS TOGETHER GREAT TASTE AND
HEALTHY GOODNESS TO MAKE
FRESH, SATISFYING AND TASTY
SALADS AND SIDES THAT ARE
PACKED WITH FULL-ON FLAVOR.

GRANDMA'S CALICO BAKED BEANS

JULIE HARRIS
BOILING SPRINGS, SC

I have fond memories of helping my grandma make this delicious dish the night before a church potluck. She would tie one of her big aprons on me and roll up my sleeves, so I could help make the sauce. As a newlywed I now make this for my own family and our church potlucks, and I am always reminded of those special times helping Grandma in the kitchen.

1/2 lb. bacon, diced
1 lb. ground beef
1/2 c. onion, chopped
1 clove garlic, minced
1/2 c. brown sugar, packed
1/2 c. catsup
1/4 c. water
1 T. cider vinegar
1 t. salt
1 t. mustard
Optional: 1/8 t. smoke-flavored cooking sauce
21-oz. can pork & beans
16-oz. can kidney beans, drained and rinsed
16-oz. can Great Northern beans, drained and rinsed

In a large skillet, cook bacon over medium heat until crisp. Remove bacon to paper towels; discard drippings. In the same skillet, brown beef, onion and garlic; drain. In a large bowl, whisk together brown sugar, catsup, water, vinegar, salt, mustard and sauce, if using. Add beans, crumbled bacon and beef mixture; stir well. Spoon mixture into a greased 2-quart casserole dish. Bake, uncovered, at 325 degrees for 45 to 60 minutes, until beans are bubbly and as thick as desired. May also be cooked in a slow cooker. Cover and cook on high setting for 2 to 3 hours, or on low setting for 5 to 6 hours.

Makes 10 to 15 servings.

BEST BROCCOLI CASSEROLE

NANCY KAISER
YORK, SC

We have this casserole at every holiday meal. It's amazing!

In a large saucepan over medium heat, cover broccoli with water. Cook until tender; drain and transfer to an ungreased 13"x9" baking pan. In the same saucepan, melt 4 tablespoons butter. Add flour and salt; mix well. Add milk, stirring constantly, until mixture is thick and bubbly. Reduce heat; add cream cheese and stir until smooth. Pour butter mixture over broccoli; mix lightly. Top with Cheddar cheese. Melt remaining butter and toss with bread crumbs; sprinkle over top. Bake, uncovered, at 350 degrees for 40 to 50 minutes, until heated through.

Serves 6 to 8.

- 1 to 2 lbs. broccoli, chopped
- 6 T. butter, divided
- 1/4 c. all-purpose flour
- 1/4 t. salt
- 2 c. milk
- 8-oz. pkg. cream cheese, cubed
- 1 c. shredded Cheddar cheese
- 2 c. soft bread crumbs

MARSHA'S ZUCCHINI-TOMATO BAKE

MARSHA KENT
CHAPIN, SC

This side dish is easy to prepare, yet always gets great compliments at gatherings.

Arrange zucchini slices in a lightly greased 13"x9" baking pan; top with tomatoes. Drizzle tomatoes with olive oil; sprinkle with Parmesan cheese and herbs. Bake, uncovered, at 350 degrees for 35 to 45 minutes.

Serves 4 to 6.

- 4 zucchini, sliced 1/2-inch thick
- 4 tomatoes, cubed
- 1 T. olive oil
- 1/4 c. shredded Parmesan cheese
- Herbes de Provence or dried thyme to taste

RAINBOW ROTINI SALAD

ZOE BENNETT
COLUMBIA, SC

Perfect for picnics! Make it the night before and pack it to go.

12-oz. pkg. rainbow
rotini pasta, uncooked

1/2 c. green pepper,
chopped

1/2 c. red pepper,
chopped

1/2 c. red onion, chopped

1/2 c. celery, chopped

1/2 c. carrot, peeled and
cut into very thin
strips

1/2 c. sliced black olives,
drained

1/4 lb. Cheddar cheese,
diced

1 c. ranch salad
dressing

Cook pasta according to package directions; drain and rinse with cold water. Place pasta in a large serving bowl; add vegetables and cheese. Drizzle with salad dressing; toss well. Cover and chill 8 hours to overnight.

Serves 8.

HOLIDAY PEAR SALAD

**JOANN
GOOSEBERRY PATCH**

This fresh, festive salad is easy to toss together.

Toss together all ingredients in a salad bowl. Toss to mix well; serve immediately.

Makes 6 to 8 servings.

4 c. mixed salad greens

2 Anjou or Bosc pears, cored and cut into bite-size pieces

1 red onion, thinly sliced

1/2 c. crumbled blue cheese

1/2 c. balsamic vinaigrette salad dressing

DINNERTIME CONVERSATION

Most likely the only property in the country that is deeded to God, Healing Springs is a natural artesian spring that is visited for its waters that are said to have healing powers. During the Revolutionary War, wounded British soldiers were left to die. They were nursed back to health with the help of the waters and the local Native Americans. The soldiers were eventually healthy enough to rejoin their regiment in the Charleston area. Today, Healing Springs still attracts visitors to partake of the waters.

NANA'S CORNBREAD DRESSING

GLENDA TOLBERT
MOORE, SC

This is my great-grandmother's dressing, and it's delicious. While it bakes, the aroma fills the kitchen...yum! If you prefer, you can use the yellow cornbread mix that comes in the little box.

6 slices whole-wheat bread, crumbled

1-1/4 c. onion, finely chopped

1 c. celery, finely chopped

1-1/2 t. ground sage

1 t. salt

pepper to taste

3 eggs, beaten

4 c. chicken broth

Optional: 2 T. butter, melted

BUTTERMILK CORNBREAD:

2 c. self-rising buttermilk cornmeal

1-3/4 c. buttermilk or milk

1/4 c. oil

1 egg, beaten

Optional: 1 to 2 T. sugar

Bake Buttermilk Cornbread the day before. Crumble cornbread and place in a large bowl; add crumbled wheat bread and toss to mix. Add onion, celery and seasonings; beat in eggs. Gradually stir in chicken broth and mash well; consistency should be thin. Spread in a greased 13"x9" baking pan. Drizzle with butter, if using. Bake, uncovered, at 350 degrees for one hour.

Makes 16 servings.

Buttermilk Cornbread:
Combine all ingredients in a bowl; mix well. Pour batter into a 9" pie plate. Bake at 425 degrees for 25 to 30 minutes, until golden.

OLD SOUTHERN-STYLE POTATO SALAD

ZOE BENNETT
COLUMBIA, SC

We love to grill these sandwiches practically year 'round in our backyard fire ring. You can also slide the foil-wrapped sandwich onto a baking sheet and bake it at 350 degrees until hot.

Bring a large stockpot of water to boil over high heat. Add potatoes and cook for approximately 10 minutes or until tender. Drain; allow potatoes to cool. While potatoes are cooling, combine mayonnaise, mustard, onion, pickles, pickle juice, hard-boiled eggs, salt and pepper in a large bowl and mix well. Fold cooled potatoes into mayonnaise mixture and garnish with paprika.

Serves 10 to 12.

3 pounds russet potatoes, peeled and cubed

4 hard-boiled eggs, peeled and chopped

1/4 c. dill pickles, chopped

1 T. dill pickle juice

1/4 c. sweet pickles, chopped

1 T. sweet pickle juice

1/2 c. yellow onion, fincly minced

1 c. mayonnaise

1/1 c. mustard

1/2 t. sea salt

1/4 t. pepper

Garnish: paprika

PENNSYLVANIA DUTCH FILLING

BETHANNA KORTIE
GREER, SC

My husband craves this dressing almost as much as the turkey at Thanksgiving and Christmas! I save the ends of my bread in the freezer all year long to make this recipe. Serve with roast turkey and plenty of gravy.

2 sliced loaves white bread
1 c. butter
1-1/2 onions, diced
6 stalks celery, diced
2 t. poultry seasoning
2 t. garlic salt
2 t. pepper
6 eggs, beaten
Optional: chicken broth or milk

Lay out bread slices on the countertop overnight to dry out slightly. Tear bread into bite-size pieces; divide between 2 large bowls and set aside. Melt butter in a skillet over medium heat; add onions, celery and seasonings. Sauté until onions are translucent; cool to room temperature. Divide eggs between bowls; divide onion mixture between bowls. Mix with your hands until bread is slightly moistened. For a moister filling, stir in milk or broth as desired. Butter two 20-inch pieces of aluminum foil. Form filling into 2 loaves; place one loaf on each piece of foil. Fold ends of foil over the loaves and seal. Bake at 350 degrees for one hour. Remove foil; slice filling to serve.

Makes 10 servings.

CREAMY BROCCOLI CASSEROLE

**DEBRA JOHNSON
MYRTLE BEACH, SC**

A deliciously simple side dish to take to family dinners...there's never any left!

In a bowl, combine all ingredients. Spoon into a greased slow cooker. Cover and cook on low setting for 4 hours.

Makes 6 to 8 servings.

10-oz. pkg. frozen chopped broccoli, cooked and drained

1 medium onion, diced

8-oz. jar sliced mushrooms, drained

1/2 c. butter, melted

1-1/3 c. cooked rice

8-oz. jar pasteurized process cheese sauce

10-3/4 oz. can cream of mushroom soup

SOUTHERN-STYLE CABBAGE

**PATRICIA CHERRY
ROCK HILL, SC**

Each year at Christmas, my nephew, Ray, always asks for my cabbage casserole. I can't seem to make enough of them!

Spray a 13"x9" baking pan with non-stick vegetable spray. Place half the cabbage into pan; top with half the onion. Spread one can of soup over onion; repeat layers. Sprinkle with cheese. Bake, uncovered, at 350 degrees for 40 to 45 minutes, or until cabbage is tender.

Serves 6 to 8.

1 head cabbage, quartered

1 onion, sliced and divided

2 10-3/4 oz. cans cream of mushroom soup

8-oz. pkg. shredded Cheddar cheese

BARBECUED GREEN BEANS

**ZOE BENNETT
COLUMBIA, SC**

The tangy flavor makes these beans a great side with grilled meats. It's all done on the stovetop...convenient when the oven is in use.

4 slices bacon, chopped
1/4 c. white vinegar
1/2 c. sugar
1/2 c. brown sugar, packed
4 14-1/2 oz. cans green beans
salt and pepper to taste

In a large saucepan over medium heat, cook bacon until crisp. Remove bacon to paper towels; drain pan. Add vinegar and sugars to same pan; bring to a boil over medium heat. Add 2 undrained cans of beans to pan; drain remaining beans and add. Stir in crumbled bacon; season with salt and pepper. Bring to a boil over medium heat; reduce heat to medium-low. Simmer for about 20 minutes, stirring occasionally, until sauce is thickened and flavors have blended, about 20 minutes.

Serves 8.

THE BAY'S PEPPER SLAW

**TONI CURRIN
DILLON, SC**

A crunchy, fresh-tasting coleslaw that's a nice change from mayonnaise-based slaws.

2 c. green cabbage, shredded
1/2 c. red cabbage, shredded
1/2 c. carrots, peeled and shredded
1/2 c. green pepper, minced
2 T. sugar
1/2 T. olive oil
1 t. salt
1 t. pepper

Combine cabbage, carrots and green pepper in a serving bowl; set aside. Mix remaining ingredients in a separate bowl. Pour over cabbage mixture and toss to mix well. Cover and refrigerate overnight before serving.

Makes 6 servings.

CHILLED RAINBOW PASTA SALAD

NANCY KAISER
YORK, SC

This salad is fairly quick & easy to make and very tasty. Whenever I take it somewhere, someone is sure to ask for the recipe!

Cook pasta according to package directions; drain. Rinse with cold water; drain again. Mix pasta and vegetables in a large bowl; set aside. Combine remaining ingredients in a small bowl, stirring until sugar is dissolved. Pour over pasta mixture, tossing to coat evenly. Cover and refrigerate until ready to serve.

Serves 8 to 10.

- 16-oz. pkg. rainbow radiatore pasta, uncooked
- 4 green onions, chopped
- 1 green pepper, chopped
- 4 stalks celery, diced
- 2/3 c. sugar
- 1/2 c. canola oil
- 1/3 c. catsup
- 1/4 c. white wine vinegar
- 1 t. salt

YAM-A-DANDY

JUDITH GRIFFTH
GREENSVILLE, SC

One taste and you'll agree...these sweet potatoes are just dandy!

Combine all ingredients except nuts; mix well. Pour into a greased 2-quart casserole dish. Bake, uncovered, at 350 degrees for 30 minutes. Garnish with nuts, if desired.

Serves 4.

- 29-oz. can sweet potatoes, drained and mashed
- 1/2 c. sugar
- 2 eggs, beaten
- 1/2 c. butter, melted
- 1 c. light corn syrup
- Optional: chopped walnuts or pecans

ANNA RAE'S BABY LIMAS

JUANITA PROFITT
PICKENS, SC

This is for everyone who likes a little spice in their lima beans! Anna Rae is my granddaughter who loves good ol' southern cooking. She also loves any kind of vegetable, which is odd for a five-year-old!

1 c. water
1 cube chicken bouillon
16-oz. pkg. frozen baby
  lima beans
1 slice bacon, chopped
1 clove garlic, lightly
  pressed
1/8 to 1/4 t. red pepper
  flakes
1/4 c. butter, softened
salt and pepper to taste

In a saucepan over medium heat, bring water and bouillon cube to a boil; stir. Add beans, bacon, garlic and red pepper flakes. Cover and turn heat to low. Cook about 25 minutes, until beans are tender. Drain; stir in butter, salt and pepper.

Makes 5 to 6 servings.

DINNERTIME CONVERSATION

South Carolina's state tree, the Sabal Palmetto, has soft and squishy bark that is also extremely tough. The exterior bark and trunk combined to create a formidable material for fortresses. During the Revolutionary War, the trees absorbed cannon fire well.

UNFRIED REFRIED BEANS

**KRISTY MARKNERS
FORT MILL, SC**

Mexican is my favorite food of all time! This is one of my new easy slow-cooker sides. It makes a bunch and the leftovers are just as good as the first bite! If you can't find chili salt, just substitute one teaspoon salt plus 1/2 teaspoon chili powder.

Soak beans in water overnight. Drain beans and place in a slow cooker. Add water to cover 2 inches over beans. Stir in remaining ingredients. Cover and cook on high setting for 6 to 8 hours. Drain off all but about 1/4 cup water. Use an immersion blender to blend until smooth.

Serves 8.

16-oz. pkg. dried pinto
  beans, sorted and
  rinsed
4-oz. can chopped green
  chiles
1 t. chili salt

AUNT ETHEL'S KRAUT SALAD

**GLENDA BALLARD
WEST COLUMBIA, SC**

In 1974, I went with a friend from work to visit her Aunt Ethel in the hills of Tennessee and her aunt served this salad. In the past, I'd never been crazy about kraut, but this sure changed my mind. It is delicious!

Place sauerkraut in a colander; rinse well with cold water and drain. Combine sauerkraut and remaining ingredients in a large bowl; mix well. Cover and refrigerate overnight.

Serves 4 to 6.

14-1/2 oz. can
  sauerkraut, drained
1 c. green pepper,
  chopped
1 c. onion, chopped
1 c. celery, chopped
2 T. diced pimentos,
  drained
1 c. sugar
1 c. vinegar
1/2 c. oil

CREAMY CABBAGE BAKE

KIMBERLY BURDITT
SUMMERVILLE, SC

This recipe is a favorite at our family cookouts...real comfort food.

1 head cabbage, coarsely chopped
1 c. carrots, peeled and chopped
1 c. onion, chopped
10-3/4 oz. can cream of mushroom soup
1/2 c. plus 2 T. milk
1/2 t. seasoned salt
1 t. dried parsley
8-oz. pkg. shredded Swiss cheese
8-oz. pkg. shredded Parmesan cheese

Add cabbage, carrots and onion to a large saucepan of boiling water. Cook over medium-high heat untill tender; drain. Combine with remaining ingredients. Put into a greased 13"x9" baking pan. Bake, uncovered, at 350 degrees for 45 minutes.

Serves 12.

HOMESTYLE POTATO PANCAKES

KAREN SMITH
ROCK HILL, SC

The perfect side for breakfast or supper...golden and crispy!

4 c. mashed potatoes
2 eggs, beaten
2 onions, finely chopped
1 t. salt
1/2 t. pepper
4 T. olive oil

Combine potatoes, eggs and onions in a medium mixing bowl; stir well to blend. Add salt and pepper. Heat oil in a large skillet over medium heat. Drop 1/4 cupfuls potato mixture into oil, flatten each to 3/4-inch thick. Cook each patty until golden and crispy on both sides.

Makes about 6 servings.

MUST-HAVE ASPARAGUS BAKE

GLENDA BALLARD
WEST COLUMBIA, SC

My family likes this casserole so much, we've actually drawn straws to see who would get the last serving!

In a one-quart casserole dish coated with non-stick vegetable spray, layer half the asparagus, half the cheese and half the soup. Repeat layers. Top with bread crumbs; dot with butter. Bake, uncovered, at 350 degrees for 20 minutes, until golden on top and cheese is melted.

Serves 4.

15-oz. can asparagus spears, drained and divided
2 c. shredded Cheddar cheese, divided
10-3/4 oz. can cream of mushroom soup, divided
3/4 c. dry bread crumbs
1 T. butter, sliced

MUSHROOMS & PEAS RICE

DEBRA JOHNSON
MYRTLE BEACH, SC

My husband and I really enjoy this dish!

In a large skillet, sauté mushrooms in butter; set aside. In a large saucepan, heat soup and milk; bring to a boil. Add rice to soup mixture and cover. Let cook for at least 5 minutes. When the rice is tender, stir in mushrooms, peas, salt and pepper; cook over low heat until heated through.

Makes 4 to 6 servings.

8-oz. pkg. sliced mushrooms
1 T. butter
10-3/4 oz. can cream of mushroom soup
1-1/4 c. milk
1-3/4 c. instant white rice, uncooked
1-1/2 c. frozen peas, thawed
salt and pepper to taste

HERBED MASHED POTATOES

ZOE BENNETT
COLUMBIA, SC

*Filled with fresh herbs, these potatoes are just wonderful! Serve topped
with a large melting pat of butter, of course.*

6-1/2 c. potatoes, peeled
   and cubed
2 cloves garlic, halved
1/2 c. milk
1/2 c. sour cream
1 T. butter, softened
2 T. fresh parsley,
   minced
2 T. fresh oregano,
   minced
1 T. fresh thyme, minced
3/4 t. salt
1/8 t. pepper

Place potatoes and garlic in a large saucepan;
add water to cover. Bring to a boil over medium-
high heat. Reduce heat to medium; simmer for 20
minutes, or until potatoes are very tender. Drain;
return potatoes and garlic to pan. Add remaining
ingredients; beat with an electric mixer on medium
speed to desired consistency.

Serves 6 to 8.

JUST FOR FUN

The Shag is the state dance of South Carolina.
Six counts and eight steps of upbeat shuffling
make up the swing dance. The dance developed
amongst the summer workers on Myrtle Beach,
rose in popularity in the 1940s and is a national
competition today.

FESTIVE CRANBERRY– PEAR SALAD

**KAREN SMITH
ROCK HILL, SC**

A tangy dressing is combined with pears and walnuts for a refreshing tossed green salad.

Combine vinegar and cranberries in a saucepan over medium heat; cook until cranberries are tender. Remove from heat; add oil, sugar, salt and pepper. Place in a blender and process until smooth; chill. Thinly slice one pear; dice remaining pear. In a large bowl, toss together greens, diced pear, 1/2 cup walnuts and cheese. Drizzle with dressing and toss to coat. Divide among 8 salad plates; top with sliced pear and remaining nuts.

Makes 8 servings.

1/2 c. cider vinegar
1/4 c. cranberries
1/4 c. olive oil
2 t. sugar
1/8 t. salt
1/8 t. pepper
2 red pears, cored
2 heads romaine lettuce, torn into bite-size pieces
2 heads Belgian endive, chopped
1/2 c. plus 2 T. chopped walnuts, toasted and divided
1/2 c. crumbled Gorgonzola cheese

LIP-SMACKN' SPIRAL SALAD

**KAREN SMITH
ROCK HILL, SC**

So easy to make for our many church potlucks!

6-oz. pkg. rotini, cooked

2 c. plum tomatoes, chopped

1 c. frozen corn, thawed

1/2 c. green onions, sliced

4 slices of bacon, cooked and crumbled

Rinse and drain rotini with cold water; pour into a serving bowl. Add remaining ingredients; pour Basil Salad Dressing on top. Gently toss to coat; refrigerate until serving.

Makes 8 to 10 servings.

Basil Salad Dressing:
Whisk ingredients together.

BASIL SALAD DRESSING:
1/3 c. red wine vinegar
2 T. olive oil
3 T. fresh basil, chopped
2 cloves garlic, minced
1/4 c. Parmesean cheese
1/2 t. salt
1/4 t. pepper

PRESENTATION

Serve salad portions in red or yellow peppers, melon halves or tomato cups for a clever presentation...easy to serve on buffets too.

DELICIOUS VEGETABLE MEDLEY

**DEBRA JOHNSON
MYRTLE BEACH, SC**

For a colorful salad that can be made a couple hours before dinner, try this great combination of garden vegetables.

Combine first 6 ingredients in a large bowl. Mix together dressing and mustard in a separate bowl; pour over vegetables. Cover and refrigerate 2 hours to marinate.

Serves 8.

1 c. broccoli flowerets

1 c. cucumber, sliced

1 yellow pepper, sliced

1 c. cherry tomatoes, halved

3/4 c. carrots, sliced

2 T. fresh parsley, chopped

1/2 c. Italian dressing

1 T. Dijon mustard

SKILLET SQUASH SUCCOTASH

**BRENDA WELLS
SUMMERVILLE, SC**

Our gardening neighbors left a bag of squash on our doorstep every week during the summer. It amused us as we had a garden too! No matter, squash is forgiving...it can be cooked in all kinds of ways. My family was quite fond of this dish and requested it weekly.

In a skillet over medium heat, melt butter and add oil. Add squash; cook until golden. Stir in remaining ingredients. Reduce heat; cover and simmer for 20 minutes.

Makes 4 to 6 servings.

1 T. butter

1 T. oil

4 yellow squash, thinly sliced

11-oz. can corn, drained

10-oz. can diced tomatoes with green chiles

1 t. garlic powder

CRISPY GOLDEN PARMESAN POTATOES

**DEBRA JOHNSON
MYRTLE BEACH, SC**

We love potatoes! I'm always tickled to find a tasty new way to fix them. This recipe is scrumptious.

1/4 c. butter, melted and divided

1-3/4 lbs. Yukon gold potatoes, halved lengthwise

1/2 c. grated Parmesan cheese

1 t. garlic powder

Spread one tablespoon melted butter in a 13"x9" baking pan; place remaining butter in a small bowl. Mix cheese and garlic powder in a separate small bowl. Dip cut sides of potatoes into butter, then into cheese mixture. Place cut-side down in baking pan. Drizzle with any remaining butter. Bake, uncovered, at 400 degrees for 30 to 35 minutes, until tender.

Makes 6 to 8 servings.

DINNERTIME CONVERSATION

West African people arriving off the coast of the Carolinas, Georgia and Florida throughout the 18th and 19th centuries as enslaved persons, created a language called Gullah which is still being spoken today.

CRUNCHY BACON COLESLAW

**KAREN SMITH
ROCK HILL, SC**

This delicious coleslaw is sure to be invited whenever burgers or barbecue are on the menu.

Mix mayonnaise, sugar and vinegar in a large bowl. Add remaining ingredients; mix lightly. Cover and chill until serving time.

Makes 8 to 10 servings.

3/4 c. mayonnaise

1 T. sugar

1-1/2 t. cider vinegar

4 c. green cabbage, shredded

1 c. red cabbage, shredded

4 slices bacon, crisply cooked and crumbled, or 1/2 c. real bacon bits

1/2 c. chopped peanuts

FARMSTYLE GREEN BEANS

**DEBRA JOHNSON
MYRTLE BEACH, SC**

Slow-simmered fresh green beans are our treat after we've shopped at the farmers' market.

In a skillet over medium heat, sauté onion and garlic in oil for 4 to 5 minutes, until tender. Transfer mixture to a 5-quart slow cooker; add remaining ingredients. Cover and cook on low setting for 3-1/2 to 4 hours, to desired tenderness.

Serves 8.

1 yellow onion, diced

2 cloves garlic, minced

2 T. olive oil

14-oz. can chicken broth

2 lbs. fresh green beans, snapped

1/2 t. garlic salt

salt and pepper to taste

CHAPTER THREE

SASSAFRAS MOUNTAIN

Soups, Sandwiches & Breads

GATHER 'ROUND THE TABLE TOGETHER

WITH FAMILY & FRIENDS, COZY UP

WITH A BOWL OF HEARTY SOUP OR

A TASTY SANDWICH, PERFECT FOR A

BREEZY AFTERNOON ON THE PORCH.

BEAN & SAUSAGE SOUP

MARY PAIGE BOYCE
COLUMBIA, SC

I put this scrumptious soup in the slow cooker in the morning, and when I get home, I have a great nutritious supper. I like to serve bowls of it with a big square of corn bread.

48-oz. container chicken broth

16-oz. smoked pork sausage ring, cut into 8 sections

15-oz. can black beans, drained

15-oz. can pinto beans

15-oz. can black-eyed peas

1 onion, chopped

1 red pepper, chopped

1 clove garlic, chopped

2 T. sugar

salt and pepper to taste

9-oz. pkg. frozen corn

In a slow cooker, combine broth, sausage, black beans and undrained pinto beans and black-eyed peas. Add remaining ingredients except corn. Cover and cook on low setting for 8 hours. Turn to high setting and stir in corn; cover and cook one hour longer.

Serves 4 to 6.

DINNERTIME CONVERSATION

People arrived in South Carolina over 50,000 years ago. Native American tribes such as the Cherokee, Creek and Santee have lived here for thousands of years.

DEE'S CAROLINA SEAFOOD CHOWDER

DEONA RYAN
SUMMERVILLE, SC

My family loved clam chowder during the cooler weather. Living in the Carolinas, what better way to jazz up chowder than with a special mix of seafood?

In a Dutch oven over medium heat, cook bacon until almost crisp. Add onion; cook for 10 minutes, or until golden and caramelized. Drain as desired. Combine all reserved seafood liquid in a 2-cup measuring cup. Add water if needed to equal 2 cups; add to pan. Set aside seafood. Stir in potatoes; simmer until tender. Add reserved seafood; simmer over low heat for about 5 minutes. In a bowl, add cornstarch to half-and-half and stir until dissolved. Add to chowder and cook for about 5 minutes, until beginning to thicken. Serve with oyster crackers on the side.

Makes 8 servings.

1 lb. bacon, diced

1 onion, diced

6-oz. can chopped clams, drained and liquid reserved

6-oz. can small shrimp, drained and liquid reserved

6-oz. can crabmeat, drained and liquid reserved

4 to 6 redskin potatoes, diced

1 T. cornstarch

2 c. half-and-half

Garnish: oyster crackers

SAVORY SPINACH ROLLS

**LAURIE RUPSIS
AIKEN, SC**

I bring these to our church's potlucks but never set them out before the crowd comes in. The ladies working the kitchen seem to eat a lot of them before the potluck even starts!

2 onions, chopped
3/4 c. butter
2 10-oz. pkgs. frozen spinach
3 c. stuffing mix
6 eggs, beaten
1/2 c. shredded Parmesan cheese

In a skillet over medium heat, sauté onions in butter until tender. Cook spinach according to package directions; squeeze dry. In a bowl, combine onion mixture, spinach and remaining ingredients. Shape into 2-inch balls using a cookie scoop. Refrigerate at least one hour, until firm. Place on a lightly greased baking sheet. Bake, uncovered, at 350 degrees for 20 minutes. May be frozen unbaked; bake just before serving. Serve warm or cool.

Makes 3 dozen.

APPLE "CIDER" SOUP

**JOHN & ANNE NEWSOME
COLUMBIA, SC**

This soup tastes like a cup of hot apple cider...however, the chicken broth and five-spice powder add an interesting twist! It's refreshing served between courses of a dinner party.

3 c. chicken broth
4 c. apple juice
1/2 t. cider vinegar
1/2 t. Chinese five-spice powder
1 Gala apple, peeled, cored and diced
1 Granny Smith apple, peeled, cored and diced
1/8 t. salt
red pepper flakes to taste

In a saucepan over medium heat, combine broth, apple juice, vinegar and five-spice powder. Bring to a slow simmer. Add apples; simmer until apples are just tender. Stir in salt and red pepper flakes.

Serves 8 to 10.

CHUCK WAGON CHILI

JESI ALLEN
CLOVER, SC

A family favorite! We've made this chili often over the campfire, and it's just as good at home in the slow cooker. Perfect with a slice of cornbread and topped with some shredded cheese!

Heat oil in a large skillet over medium-high heat. Add beef and brown on all sides; drain and season with salt and pepper. Meanwhile, in a 6-quart slow cooker, combine tomato purée, picante sauce, beans, mushrooms, beer and seasonings. Add beef to slow cooker. Cover and cook on low setting for 6 to 8 hours, until beef is very tender. Serve with crackers or cornbread, topped with shredded cheese and sour cream, if desired.

Makes 6 servings.

2 T. oil

2 lbs. stew beef cubes

1 T. salt, or to taste

1 T. pepper, or to taste

2 28-oz. cans tomato purée

24-oz. jar mild or medium picante sauce

2 15-oz. cans kidney beans, drained

2 8-oz. cans sliced mushrooms, drained

12-oz. bottle beer or non-alcoholic beer

3 T. chili powder, or to taste

2 T. ground cumin, or to taste

saltine crackers or cornbread

Optional: shredded Cheddar cheese, sour cream

DAD COLE'S HEARTY BEEF STEW

BONNIE COLE
EASLEY, SC

Whenever we go to visit my father-in-law in Michigan, he makes us this wonderful stew. It's always associated with good times and laughter. He serves this with his homemade oatmeal rolls.

2 lbs. stew beef, cut into 1-1/2 inch cubes

6 to 7 potatoes, peeled and cut into 1-1/2 inch cubes

8 carrots, peeled and cut into 1-1/2 inch pieces

4 to 5 stalks celery, cut into 1-inch pieces

2 onions, cut into wedges

4-oz. can sliced mushrooms, drained

1-1/2 t. dried thyme

1 t. sugar

2 bay leaves

1 cube beef bouillon

1-1/2 t. salt

1/3 c. instant tapioca, uncooked

3 c. tomato juice

In a Dutch oven, layer beef and vegetables. Sprinkle with thyme and sugar; tuck in bay leaves and bouillon cube. Add salt to tapioca; sprinkle over all. Drizzle tomato juice over everything. Cover and bake at 300 degrees for 3 hours, stirring occasionally, until beef and vegetables are tender. Discard bay leaves before serving. If made ahead and refrigerated, stew will thicken; add additional tomato juice or water when reheating.

Serves 6 to 8.

GRILLED FLANK STEAK SANDWICH

VALERIE GARDNER
LYMAN, SC

I've been making these hearty sandwiches for years, grilling the steak in the backyard and then finishing the sandwiches indoors. On a hot summer's evening, it's nice to keep the kitchen cool!

On a gas or charcoal grill, cook steak to desired doneness; add seasonings. Let steak rest for about 10 minutes; slice thinly on the diagonal. In a skillet over medium-high heat, sauté onion and pepper, if desired, in oil until caramelized. Spread mayonnaise on one side of bread. Assemble sandwiches with bread, sliced steak, onion mixture and cheese. Spread outside of sandwiches with a little butter. Heat a countertop grill, panini press or grill pan. Grill until toasted and cheese is melted.

Serves 4 to 6.

1 to 1-1/2 lb. beef flank steak
seasoned salt and pepper to taste
1 sweet onion, thinly sliced
Optional: 1 green or red pepper, thinly sliced
2 to 3 t. olive oil
mayonnaise to taste
1 loaf sliced bread
4 to 6 slices provolone cheese
softened butter to taste

DINNERTIME CONVERSATION

South Carolina is one of the nation's top producers of kaolin (natural clay), mica and vermiculite, a mineral that's often used for insulation or for growing plants.

KIELBASA CAMP STEW

VICI RANDOLPH
GAFFNEY, SC

I love this recipe! It is so simple, but filling and delicious. This stew is terrific with some crusty bread or cornbread.

1 lb. Kielbasa sausage, cut into 1-inch slices

3 14-1/2 oz. cans diced tomatoes

2 12-oz. pkgs. frozen shoepeg corn

4 potatoes, peeled and diced

1/2 head cabbage, coarsely chopped

1 t. Cajun seasoning or other spicy seasoning

salt to taste

Combine Kielbasa, undrained tomatoes and remaining ingredients in a Dutch oven; cover with water. Simmer over medium-high heat until potatoes are tender, stirring occasionally, about 30 minutes.

Makes 6 to 8 servings.

SLOW-COOKER WHITE CHICKEN CHILI

NANCY LANNING
LANCASTER, SC

While our daughter was babysitting a family, they served white chili. It has now become a favorite of our family too!

48-oz. jar Great Northern beans

16-oz. jar mild, medium or hot salsa

1/2 t. garlic, minced

2-1/2 c. cooked chicken, chopped

16-oz. pkg. mozzarella cheese, diced

Combine all ingredients in a 5-quart slow cooker; stir well. Cover and cook on low setting for 4 to 5 hours, until hot and cheese is melted.

Serves 6.

HARVEST BREAD

NANCY LANNING
LANCASTER, SC

My grandmother had this recipe in a little booklet from her Women's Missionary Association years ago, and I have made this bread so often. It's a favorite of ours!

Combine sugar, oil, eggs and vanilla in a large bowl. Beat thoroughly with an electric mixer on medium speed; set aside. In another bowl, mix together flour, baking powder, baking soda, salt and cinnamon; add to sugar mixture and stir well. Fold in carrots, zucchini and apple. Pour batter into a greased and floured 13"x9" baking pan. Bake at 350 degrees for 35 to 45 minutes. Cool; spread with Cream Cheese Frosting and sprinkle with pecans. Cut into squares.

Makes 12 to 15 servings.

Cream Cheese Frosting:
Combine cream cheese, milk and vanilla; beat together. Gradually beat in powdered sugar until smooth.

1-1/3 c. sugar
1-1/3 c. oil
3 eggs
2 t. vanilla extract
2 c. all-purpose flour
1 t. baking powder
1 t. baking soda
1 t. salt
2 t. cinnamon
1 c. carrots, peeled and shredded
1-1/2 c. zucchini, shredded
1 c. apple, peeled, cored and chopped
Garnish: chopped pecans

Cream Cheese Frosting:
2 3-oz. pkgs. cream cheese, softened
2 t. vanilla extract
16-oz. pkg. powdered sugar
1 T. milk

LAURIE'S LEMON BREAD

LAURIE RUPSIS
AIKEN, SC

Someone once told me this recipe should be included on my resume! It's supposed to taste even better after sitting for a day. Good luck with that...mine has never lasted that long, as my husband can eat the whole loaf! By the way, 3 tablespoons lemon extract may seem like a lot, but trust me, that's correct.

1-1/2 c. sugar, divided
1/3 c. butter, melted
3 T. lemon extract
2 eggs, beaten
1/2 c. milk
1-1/2 c. all-purpose flour
1 t. baking powder
1-1/2 t. lemon zest
Optional: 1/2 c. chopped nuts
1/4 c. lemon juice

In a large bowl, mix one cup sugar and remaining ingredients except lemon juice. Pour batter into a greased and floured 9"x5" loaf pan. Bake at 350 degrees for 50 to 60 minutes. Cool 10 minutes; turn out loaf onto a piece of aluminum foil. For glaze, stir together lemon juice and remaining sugar. Drizzle glaze over loaf. For best flavor, wrap loaf in foil or plastic wrap; let stand one day before slicing.

Makes one loaf.

CREAM CHEESE BISCUITS

ZOE BENNETT
COLUMBIA, SC

We love these oh-so-easy biscuits warm, spread with plenty of butter! To save time, just cut the dough into 12 squares.

2-1/2 c. biscuit baking mix
2 T. butter, chilled
1/4 c. cream cheese, chilled
3/4 c. milk

Add baking mix to a large bowl; use a fork to cut in cream cheese and butter. Add milk; stir just until combined. Knead dough 2 to 3 times on a floured surface. Roll out into a rectangle, 3/4-inch thick. Cut into 12 biscuits with a biscuit cutter; place on a parchment paper-lined baking sheet. Bake at 450 degrees for 10 to 12 minutes, until lightly golden.

Makes one dozen.

PATCHWORK MUFFINS

TONI CURRIN
DILLON, SC

A little of this, a little of that and you have the most tasty muffins!

Mix together flour, cranberries, baking powder, baking soda, spices and salt; set aside. Stir together remaining ingredients except chocolate chips; blend with flour mixture. Spoon into greased muffin cups filling 2/3 full; bake at 375 degrees for 15 to 18 minutes. Place chocolate chips in a plastic zipping bag; microwave on high setting until chocolate is melted, stirring every 15 seconds. Snip a small corner off bag; drizzle over muffins.

Makes 1-1/2 dozen.

2 c. all-purpose flour

3/4 c. sweetened, dried cranberries

1 t. baking powder

1/2 t. baking soda

1/2 t. cinnamon

1/2 t. ground cloves

1/4 t. nutmeg

1/4 t. salt

3/4 c. whipping cream

1/2 c. milk

2 eggs, beaten

1/2 c. brown sugar, packed

1/2 t. vanilla extract

1 c. canned pumpkin

1/4 c. butter, melted

1-1/4 c. semi-sweet chocolate chips

COFFEE CAN BREAD

**LAURIE RUPSIS
AIKEN, SC**

When our children were still at home, I baked this bread in a big coffee can. Now that we're empty nesters, I use soup cans and get five loaves. We can enjoy one and freeze the others for later!

1-1/2 c. raisins
2 c. hot water
2 T. butter, sliced
2 t. baking soda
4 c. all-purpose flour
2 c. sugar
2 eggs, beaten
1 t. cinnamon
1 t. vanilla extract
Optional: 1 c. chopped nuts
Garnish: softened cream cheese

Combine raisins, hot water, butter and baking soda in a large bowl. Cover and let stand at room temperature, 8 hours to overnight. Add remaining ingredients except cream cheese; mix well until a very thick batter forms. Grease and flour three, one-pound metal coffee cans, or five, 10-3/4 ounce soup cans. Spoon batter into cans, filling 1/2 full. Bake at 350 degrees, 50 to 60 minutes for coffee cans, or 40 to 45 minutes for soup cans. Serve warm or at room temperature with cream cheese.

Makes 3 regular loaves or 5 mini loaves.

EASY CHEESY BISCUITS

**VICKIE
GOOSEBERRY PATCH**

Better than my favorite restaurant biscuit!

10-oz. tube refrigerated flaky biscuits
8-oz. pkg. Cheddar cheese, sliced into 10 cubes
1 T. milk
1 t. poppy seed

Separate dough into 10 biscuits. Open a small pocket in side of each biscuit; tuck a cheese cube into each pocket. Press dough together to seal well. Place biscuits on an ungreased baking sheet. Cut a deep "X" in top of each biscuit. Brush with milk and sprinkle with poppy seed. Bake at 400 degrees for 10 to 12 minutes, until golden. Serve warm.

Makes 10 biscuits.

COMFORT CHICKEN NOODLE SOUP

TINA QUINNELLY
COWPENS, SC

This simple recipe is a favorite of my family. Sure to warm you on chilly autumn evenings!

In a soup pot over medium-high heat, combine water and bouillon cubes; bring to a boil. Add half of noodles; reserve remaining noodles for another recipe. Cook for 10 minutes, or until noodles are tender. Do not drain. Stir in soup and chicken; heat through. Remove from heat; stir in sour cream.

Makes 8 servings.

8 c. water

8 cubes chicken bouillon

12-oz. pkg. egg noodles, uncooked and divided

10-3/4 oz. can cream of chicken soup

3 c. cooked chicken, cubed

8-oz. container sour cream

TOMATO & BASIL BISQUE

DEBRA JOHNSON
MYRTLE BEACH, SC

Garnish servings with a swirl of cream and a sprig of basil leaves.

In a large saucepan over medium heat, sauté onions and carrots in butter until tender. Stir in tomatoes, sugar, salt and pepper; bring to a boil. Reduce heat; cover and simmer for 10 minutes. Cool soup slightly; transfer to a blender. Add basil; cover and process until smooth. Pour soup back into saucepan. Stir in broth; heat through.

Serves 4.

2 onions, chopped

2 carrots, peeled and shredded

1 T. butter

8 tomatoes, peeled and chopped

1/2 t. sugar

1/2 t. salt

1/4 t. pepper

1/2 c. fresh basil, chopped

2 c. chicken broth

GRANDADDY'S SKILLET CORNBREAD

**JENNIFER AUSTIN
HEATH SPRINGS, SC**

This recipe was handed down from my grandaddy to my mother and now to me. This is the easiest and best-tasting cornbread. It's crispy and buttery on the outside...soft and moist inside. We eat it year 'round with soup. It's great for making cornbread dressing too.

2 c. self-rising cornmeal
   mix
2 T. butter, melted and
   cooled slightly
2 c. buttermilk
2 eggs, beaten
2 T. mayonnaise
1 T. shortening

In a bowl, combine all ingredients except shortening. Stir until creamy. Grease a cast-iron skillet well with shortening. Pour batter into skillet. Bake at 425 degrees for 15 minutes, or until a toothpick inserted in the center tests clean. Cut into wedges; serve warm.

Makes 8 servings.

AZTEC CORN CHOWDER

**VICKIE
GOOSEBERRY PATCH**

I love this soup with all my favorite flavors!

1/4 c. butter
3-1/2 c. corn
1 clove garlic, minced
1 c. chicken broth
2 c. milk
1 t. dried oregano
4-oz. can diced green
   chiles
1 c. shredded Monterey
   Jack cheese
salt to taste
Optional: chopped
   tomato, chopped
   cilantro

Melt butter in a large saucepan over medium heat. Add corn and garlic; heat and stir until corn is heated through. Remove from heat. Place broth and 2 cups corn mixture into a blender. Cover and blend until smooth; stir into mixture in saucepan. Add milk, oregano and chiles and mix well; bring to a boil over medium heat, stirring constantly. Remove from heat; stir in cheese and salt to taste. Garnish with tomato and cilantro, if desired.

Makes 4 to 6 servings.

YELLOW BOWL CLOVERLEAF ROLLS

**MONICA WILKINSON
BURTON, SC**

This recipe has been popular in our family for four generations! My mom remembers my grandma making these in a yellow mixing bowl. Mom continued that tradition and made hers in a yellow bowl too. I can still see the dough rising up over the top in the refrigerator.

Pour warm water, about 110 to 115 degrees, into a large bowl. Add yeast and one teaspoon sugar; stir to dissolve. Mix in milk, salt, remaining sugar and oil. Add eggs, beating well. Add enough flour to make a soft dough; let stand for 10 minutes. Knead until smooth and elastic, adding flour as needed. Place in a large greased bowl; cover with a tea towel and refrigerate overnight. Spray muffin tins with non-stick vegetable spray. Shape dough into one-inch balls; place 3 balls into each muffin cup. Cover; let rise until double in bulk. Bake at 400 degrees for 15 to 20 minutes.

Makes about 3-1/2 dozen.

1 c. warm water
2 envs. active dry yeast
3/4 c. plus 1 t. sugar, divided
2 c. warm milk
4 t. salt
2/3 c. oil
2 eggs, beaten
10 to 11 c. all-purpose flour

KITCHEN TIP

To bring honey back to a drizzly state: Place the container in a bowl of hot water until the honey is smooth and runny.

SHARON'S BANANA MUFFINS

SHARON WOOD
WEST COLUMBIA, SC

I have used this recipe since my daughter was a baby...she enjoyed making these herself when I was teaching her to cook. She is now 29 years old and her children are learning to bake under my supervision too. Enjoy making your own memories!

1/2 c. butter, softened
1 c. sugar
2 eggs, beaten
3/4 c. ripe banana, mashed
1-1/4 c. all-purpose flour
3/4 t. baking soda
1/2 t. salt

Blend butter and sugar; add eggs and beat well. Stir in banana; set aside. Sift together flour, baking soda and salt; add to butter mixture and mix until moistened. Fill paper-lined muffin cups 2/3 full. Bake at 350 degrees for 25 to 30 minutes. If preferred, use a greased and floured 9"x5" baking pan; bake for an additional 5 to 10 minutes.

Makes 8 to 10 muffins or one loaf.

PINEAPPLE NUT LOAF

KAREN SMITH
ROCK HILL, SC

When I was growing up, I loved to give little tea parties for my dolls. Mom would bake this sweet, tender bread for me to serve with cream cheese...so dainty! Now I bake it for my own little girl.

2-3/4 c. all-purpose flour
3/4 c. sugar
1 T. baking powder
3/4 t. salt
1 c. crushed pineapple, drained
1 c. chopped dates
1 c. chopped walnuts
1 egg, beaten
1/3 c. milk
1/3 c. butter, melted

In a bowl, mix together flour, sugar, baking powder and salt. In a separate bowl, combine remaining ingredients. Add pineapple mixture to flour mixture; stir until moistened. Pour into a well greased and floured 32-ounce metal coffee can; cover with aluminum foil. Place in a slow cooker. Cover and cook on high setting for 3 to 4 hours, until loaf tests done with a toothpick inserted in the center. Remove can to a wire rack; uncover and let stand for 5 minutes. Turn out loaf onto wire rack; cool.

Makes one loaf.

WHITE BEAN SOUP

PAIGE BEAR
LYMAN, SC

*My girls love this soup on a cold day. I serve it with grilled ham sandwiches.
It's equally good topped with herbed croutons.*

In a soup pot, sauté onion in olive oil over medium-high heat. Add garlic; cook and stir for 30 seconds. Sprinkle with flour; cook and stir until flour is blended with onion mixture. Whisk in chicken broth; add beans and rosemary. Bring to a boil over medium heat; reduce heat to medium-low. Simmer for 30 minutes, stirring occasionally. At serving time, discard rosemary sprig; season with salt and pepper.

Makes 6 servings.

1/3 c. white onion, chopped

2 T. olive oil

1 clove garlic, minced

3 T. all-purpose flour or rice flour

2 14-1/2 oz. cans chicken broth

2 16-oz. cans white beans, drained and rinsed

4-inch sprig fresh rosemary

1/4 t. kosher salt

1/4 t. pepper

PRESENTATION

Simple garnishes dress up main dishes all year 'round! Fresh mint sprigs add coolness and color to summertime dishes, while rosemary sprigs and cranberries add a festive touch to holiday platters.

LILLIAN'S BEEF STEW

**NANCY DYNES
GOOSE CREEK, SC**

*My mother made this for us when we were small children and now
I make it for my own family. It's a wonderful dinner to come home
to on a cold day.*

2 lbs. stew beef cubes

2 potatoes, peeled and
quartered

3 stalks celery, diced

4 carrots, peeled and
thickly sliced

2 onions, quartered

2 c. cocktail vegetable
juice

1/3 c. quick-cooking
tapioca, uncooked

1 T. sugar

1 T. salt

1/2 t. dried basil

1/4 t. pepper

Arrange beef and vegetables in slow cooker.
Combine remaining ingredients; pour into slow
cooker. Cover and cook on low setting for 8 to
10 hours.

Serves 8.

ITALIAN MEATBALL SUBS

CLYDIA MIMS
EFFINGHAM, SC

This recipe is so good! I like to make a double batch and freeze half for another meal...the meatballs are good over pasta too!

Combine all ingredients except buns and mozzarella in a large bowl; mix well. Form into 2-inch balls; place in a slow cooker. Spoon Sauce over top. Cover and cook on low setting for 6 to 8 hours. Place 3 to 4 meatballs on each bun; top with sauce and mozzarella.

Makes 8 sandwiches.

Sauce:
Mix all ingredients in a saucepan over medium heat; simmer until heated through.

1 lb. ground beef

1 c. Italian-seasoned dry
  bread crumbs

1/2 c. grated Parmesan
  cheese

1 T. fresh parsley,
  minced

1 clove garlic, minced

1/2 c. milk

1 egg

1-1/2 t. salt

1/2 t. pepper

8 sub buns, split

Garnish: shredded
  mozzarella cheese

SAUCE:

28-oz. can tomato purée

28-oz. can Italian-style
  crushed tomatoes

1/2 c. grated Parmesan
  cheese

2 1-1/2 oz. pkgs.
  spaghetti sauce mix

salt and pepper to taste

DRESSED OYSTER PO'BOYS

KAREN SMITH
ROCK HILL, SC

These sandwiches are piled high with plump fried oysters and slaw, all atop a tangy sauce. Mmm...it's good!

1-1/2 c. self-rising cornmeal

1-1/2 T. salt-free Cajun seasoning, divided

2 12-oz. containers fresh shucked oysters, drained

peanut or vegetable oil for frying

1 c. mayonnaise, divided

2 T. Dijon mustard

2 T. white vinegar

6 c. finely shredded multicolored cabbage

2 T. catsup

1 T. prepared horseradish

3/4 t. paprika

4 hoagie rolls, split and toasted

Combine cornmeal and one tablespoon Cajun seasoning; dredge oysters in mixture. Pour oil into a Dutch oven to a depth of 2 inches and put on medium heat. Heat to 375 degrees. Fry oysters, in 3 batches, 2 to 3 minutes or until golden. Drain on wire racks. For slaw, stir together 1/2 cup mayonnaise, mustard and vinegar. Stir in cabbage; set slaw aside. Stir together remaining mayonnaise, catsup, horseradish, Cajun seasoning and paprika. Spread bottom halves of rolls with mayonnaise mixture. Layer with oysters and top with slaw; cover with roll tops.

Serves 4.

JUST FOR FUN

Raven Cliff Falls is the highest waterfall in the state. At its peak, water cascades over 400 feet into a deep pool below. Several different walking paths will take you to the top or bottom of the falls.

3-DAY VEGETABLE STEW

BRENDA WELLS
SUMMERVILLE, SC

Summer finds us with a lot of fresh veggies on hand! Between my own garden and neighbors who would leave bags of veggies on the porch, we needed to find different ways to use them while they were fresh. I decided a stew would keep us happy. We make this on Sunday evenings so my husband can take some to work. Especially good in cold weather.

In a stockpot, combine beef broth, onions, potatoes, carrots, corn, green beans, tomatoes with juice and seasonings. Bring to a boil over high heat. Reduce heat to low; cover with a vented lid. Simmer for about 30 minutes, skimming any foam that may rise to the top. Add zucchini, squash, celery and green pepper; simmer for 15 minutes. Add cabbage; cook about 10 minutes. For a thicker soup, dissolve cornstarch in cold water; add to stew and cook until thickened. Tastes best the next day and keeps well in refrigerator; reheat only the amount desired.

Makes 16 servings.

2 32-oz. containers beef broth
2 onions, diced
3 potatoes, peeled and cut into 1-inch cubes
1 lb. baby carrots, sliced
2 11-oz. cans corn, drained
16-oz. can green beans, drained
15-1/2 oz. can petite diced tomatoes
1 T. garlic powder
1/2 t. dried thyme
1/2 t. salt
1/2 t. pepper
2 zucchini, halved lengthwise and thinly sliced
1 yellow squash, halved lengthwise and thinly sliced
3 to 4 stalks celery, chopped
1 green pepper, diced
1/2 head cabbage, shredded
1 T. cornstarch
1/4 c. cold water

SHREDDED CHICKEN SANDWICHES

VICKIE
GOOSEBERRY PATCH

Tender chicken piled high on a soft bun...just like the sandwiches at old-fashioned church socials.

1/4 c. olive oil
4 boneless, skinless chicken breasts
1 onion, chopped
10-3/4 oz. can cream of mushroom soup
1 c. chicken broth
1/2 c. sherry or chicken broth
2 t. soy sauce
2 t. Worcestershire sauce
salt and pepper to taste
sandwich buns, split
Optional: pickle slices, lettuce leaves

Heat oil in a skillet over medium-high heat. Add chicken. Cook for 5 minutes on each side, until golden. Transfer chicken to a slow cooker; set aside. Add onion to drippings in skillet. Sauté until golden; drain. Add soup, broth, sherry or broth, sauces and seasonings to skillet. Stir mixture well and spoon over chicken in slow cooker. Cover and cook on low setting for 6 to 8 hours. Shred chicken with a fork; spoon onto buns. Garnish with pickles and lettuce, if desired.

Makes 8 servings.

KITCHEN TIP

Keep your plastic wrap in the refrigerator. This will make the wrap stretch evenly and properly without sticking to itself.

PORK & GREEN CHILE STEW

**KAREN SMITH
ROCK HILL, SC**

Add more chiles if you like it extra hot...serve a basket of warm flour tortillas alongside.

In a stockpot, brown pork in oil over medium-high heat. Remove pork and set aside, reserving drippings in stockpot; increase heat to high. Add one cup broth to reserved drippings; cook and stir until boiling. Return pork to stockpot; stir in remaining ingredients and enough of remaining broth to barely cover. Reduce heat to low. Cover and simmer for 1-1/2 to 2 hours, until thickened and pork is very tender.

Makes 8 servings.

3 lbs. boneless pork loin, cubed

3 T. oil

4 c. chicken broth, divided

14-1/2 oz. can diced tomatoes

11-oz. can corn, drained

10-oz. jar green chile salsa

4-oz. can chopped green chiles

3 stalks celery, chopped

4 cloves garlic, minced

salt to taste

HEARTY HOAGIE

JOANN
GOOSEBERRY PATCH

*We love to grill these sandwiches practically year 'round in our backyard
re ring. You can also slide the foil-wrapped sandwich onto a baking sheet
and bake it at 350 degrees until hot.*

2 T. olive oil

1 T. white wine vinegar

1/3 c. fresh basil,
chopped

1 loaf French bread,
halved lengthwise

6-oz. pkg. sliced
mozzarella cheese,
divided

6-oz. pkg. sliced
pastrami

2 roma tomatoes, thinly
sliced

pepper to taste

Whisk together oil, vinegar and basil in a small bowl;
set aside. Hollow out bottom half of loaf, leaving a
1/2-inch thick shell. Layer with half of cheese, all of
the pastrami and tomatoes. Drizzle with oil mixture;
sprinkle with pepper. Layer with remaining cheese;
add top half of loaf. Wrap in aluminum foil. Grill over
medium heat for 20 to 25 minutes, turning every
5 minutes, until heated through. Slice crosswise to
serve.

Makes 4 to 6 servings.

GARLIC CHEDDAR
BISCUIT CUPS

KRISTY MARKNERS
FORT MILL, SC

*This is a super easy, fast recipe! I often spoon the batter into giant
muffin cups to make 3 oversize biscuits, and then I bake them at 350
degrees for 30 to 35 minutes.*

1 c. self-rising flour

3/4 c. fat-free
buttermilk

1/2 c. shredded Cheddar
cheese

1 t. minced roasted
garlic

Combine all ingredients in a medium bowl; mix with
a fork. Fill greased or paper-lined muffin cups
3/4 full. Bake at 425 degrees for 17 to 20 minutes,
until golden.

Makes 6.

APPLE-BARLEY SOUP

DEBRA JOHNSON
MYRTLE BEACH, SC

Fresh apples give color and a slightly sweet taste to this recipe.

Sauté onions in oil over medium heat in a small stockpot. Reduce heat; cover and cook 10 minutes, stirring occasionally, until browned. Add broth, cider, barley, carrots, thyme, marjoram and bay leaf. Cover and cook for one hour, or until barley is tender. Combine remaining ingredients in a small bowl, then add to soup; cook 5 minutes, or until apples are tender. Discard bay leaf before serving.

Makes 4 to 6 servings.

2 onions, thinly sliced
2 T. oil
3-1/2 c. vegetable broth
1-1/2 c. apple cider
1/3 c. pearled barley, uncooked
2 carrots, diced
1 t. dried thyme
1/4 t. dried marjoram
1 bay leaf
2 c. apples, cored and chopped
1/4 c. fresh parsley, minced
1 T. lemon juice
1/4 t. salt

DINNERTIME CONVERSATION

Sassafras Mountain is 3,554 feet, making it the tallest mountain in the state. Sassafras stands at the southern edge of the Appalachian Mountains and offers 360-degree views of the state.

CHAPTER FOUR

MYRTLE BEACH

Mains

FILL THEM UP WITH A STICK-TO-THE-RIBS MEAL THAT IS FULL OF FLAVOR AND HEARTY ENOUGH TO SATISFY EVEN THE BIGGEST APPETITE.

HOMETOWN CHICKEN POT PIE

**KIM WILLIAMS
WEST COLUMBIA, SC**

The crust on this pie is spooned over the filling rather than being rolled out...so easy!

3 to 4 lbs. boneless, skinless chicken breasts, cooked and cubed

2 16-oz. pkgs. frozen mixed vegetables, thawed

10-3/4 oz. can cream of chicken soup

10-3/4 oz. can cream of celery soup

1/2 c. chicken broth

1 c. biscuit baking mix

1/2 c. milk

1/2 c. margarine, melted

salt and pepper to taste

Arrange chicken in an ungreased deep 13"x9" baking pan; set aside. Mix vegetables with soups and broth; pour over chicken. Combine biscuit mix, milk and margarine; spread over filling. Add salt and pepper to taste. Bake, uncovered, at 375 degrees for one hour, until bubbly and golden.

Serves 6.

BARBECUED BEER CHICKEN

**KRISTY MARKNERS
FORT MILL, SC**

This chicken is very moist and delicious. My three-year-old son gets so excited when we buy whole chickens at the grocery store...he says "Cock-a-doodle-zoo!" all the way home!

Spray a large slow cooker with non-stick vegetable spray. Carefully loosen skin from chicken. Rub seasoning generously under and on top of skin. Place chicken in a slow cooker; pour beer over chicken. Cover and cook on low setting for 8 hours.

Serves 6.

3 to 4-lb. roasting chicken
1/4 c. barbecue seasoning
12-oz. bottle regular or non-alcoholic beer

SOUTHERN SHRIMP BOIL

**KAREN SMITH
ROCK HILL, SC**

Growing up, my family would gather with neighbors every Saturday night for a shrimp boil. We still try to carry on this tradition today.

Combine water and seasoning in a large stockpot; bring to a boil. Add potatoes and boil, covered, for 12 minutes. Add corn; boil for another 5 minutes. Add shrimp and boil until shrimp are pink, about 4 minutes. Drain and transfer mixture to a large serving bowl. Garnish as desired.

Serves 6 to 8.

6 qts. water
3/4 c. seafood seasoning
2 lbs. new redskin potatoes
2 large white onions, sliced
5 ears corn, husked and halved
2 lbs. uncooked large shrimp, cleaned
Garnish: cocktail sauce, melted butter, lemon wedges

SOUTHERN FRIED CHICKEN

DEBRA JOHNSON
MYRTLE BEACH, SC

It isn't a picnic without this crisp fried chicken! Served hot or cold, it's a delicious favorite of my whole family.

3-1/2 lbs. chicken
  breasts, thighs and
  drumsticks
1 t. paprika
1 t. garlic powder
1 t. onion powder
2 t. salt
1/2 t. pepper
2 c. all-purpose flour
4 c. canola or peanut oil
  for frying

Cut large chicken breasts in half, if using. Sprinkle chicken pieces generously with seasonings; roll in flour to coat. Set aside chicken to stand for 30 minutes. Add 3/4 inch oil to a large cast-iron skillet. Heat over medium-high heat to about 350 degrees. Carefully add chicken to skillet; do not crowd. Cover and fry until golden and chicken juices run clear when pierced, turning once, 20 to 30 minutes. Drain on a wire rack set over a baking sheet.

Serves 6.

CREAMY ITALIAN CHICKEN & NOODLES

LYNDA WILLOUGHBY
FORT MILL, SC

This recipe is very easy and kid-friendly, yet delicious enough for company. Just dress it up with a sprinkle of chopped fresh parsley.

6 boneless, skinless
  chicken thighs
2 1-oz. pkgs. zesty
  Italian salad dressing
  mix
32-oz. container chicken
  broth
2 8-oz. pkgs. cream
  cheese, cubed
16-oz. pkg. medium egg
  noodles, cooked

Place chicken thighs in a slow cooker. Sprinkle with dressing mix; pour broth over chicken. Cover and cook on low setting for 6 to 8 hours, until chicken is very tender. Remove chicken to a plate, reserving broth in slow cooker; shred chicken with a fork and set aside. Add cream cheese to broth in slow cooker; stir until melted. Add cooked noodles and shredded chicken to slow cooker; stir gently. Let stand for about 15 minutes, until thickened and creamy.

Makes 6 servings.

Apple Jack Muffins, p8

Whether you are looking for a quick breakfast to start the day off right, no-fuss party fare for those special guests, satisfying soups and sandwiches for the perfect lunch, main dishes to bring them to the table fast, or a sweet little something to savor at the end of the meal, you'll love these recipes from the amazing cooks in beautiful South Carolina.

Spinach Quiche, p9

Peachy Fruit Sorbet, p143

Sweet & Spicy Bacon, p12

Yankee Iced Tea, p114

Italian Meatball Subs, p69

Southern Shrimp Boil, p79

Yellow Bowl Cloverleaf Rolls, p65

Simply Scrumptious Sticky Wings, p105

Easy Cheesy Biscuits, p62

Grandaddy's Skillet Cornbread, p64

Cream Cheese Danish, p23

Tangy Radish Bites, p115

Rainbow Rotini Salad, p32

Cheddar Fondue, p117

Grandma's Calico Baked Beans, p30

Karen's French Apple Pie, p141

Skillet Squash Succotash, p47

Chicken Lasagna with
Roasted Red Pepper Sauce, p110

Barbecued Beer Chicken, p79

Upside-Down Apple-Pecan Pie, p130

Hometown Chicken Pot Pie, p78

SPEEDY CHICKEN-BROCCOLI ALFREDO

SHERI WEST
YORK, SC

I came up with this recipe one night when I was short on time. My two teenagers were super hungry and needed to leave the house again quickly for the homecoming football game and the marching band that would perform at the game. It was a success!

Cook pasta according to package directions, adding broccoli to cooking pot; drain. Meanwhile, heat oil in a large skillet over medium heat. Add chicken; cook until chicken juices run clear. Drain; stir in soup, sauce and cheese. Add pasta mixture; stir gently until coated with sauce.

Makes 8 servings.

- 16-oz. pkg. rotini pasta, uncooked
- 1 bunch broccoli, cut into flowerets
- 3 boneless, skinless chicken breasts, sliced
- 1 to 2 T. olive oil
- 10-3/4 oz. can reduced-fat cream of chicken soup
- 16-oz. jar roasted garlic Parmesan Alfredo sauce
- 1 c. shredded Italian-blend cheese
- salt and pepper to taste

JUST FOR FUN

Bowman is home to the UFO Welcome Center. Here, aliens and travelers alike can tour the center and stop for a rest.

TERIYAKI ORANGE ROAST CHICKEN

LAURIE RUPSIS
AIKEN, SC

I don't know where I found this recipe, but I'm glad I did! It has become my go-to special dish.

3-1/2 lb. roasting chicken

3/4 c. teriyaki sauce

1/4 c. orange juice

1/4 c. orange marmalade

2 T. olive oil

6 cloves garlic, finely sliced

1/2 lb. green beans, trimmed

6 green onions, green part only, cut into large pieces

2 bay leaves

3 large pieces orange zest, white pith removed

Pat chicken dry. Tuck wings under and tie legs together with kitchen twine; set aside. In a small bowl, combine teriyaki sauce, orange juice and orange marmalade; set aside. Heat oil in a Dutch oven over medium-high heat. Add garlic; sauté for 2 minutes. Add beans and onions. Cook for 4 minutes, stirring often. Remove pan from heat; push vegetables to one side. Add chicken to pan; brush thoroughly with sauce mixture. Add bay leaves and orange zest to pan. Bake, uncovered, at 375 degrees for about one hour, basting with sauce every 15 minutes, until chicken juices run clear when pierced. Check for doneness after one hour. Turn off oven; allow chicken to rest in oven with the door slightly open for about 15 minutes. Discard bay leaves and zest. Carve chicken; serve with beans and onions.

Makes 6 to 8 servings.

CHICKEN PICCATA

A.M. GILSTRAP
EASLEY, SC

*As children we always requested our favorite, "Flattened Chicken,"
because Mom used a mallet to pound the chicken flat. She always said it
was a good recipe to relieve stress! Cooked rice goes very well with this.*

Flatten chicken between 2 layers of plastic wrap with a mallet; sprinkle with pepper and garlic powder. Whisk egg and milk together. Dip chicken in egg mixture; coat with bread crumbs. Melt margarine and oil in a skillet over medium heat. Sauté chicken for 4 to 5 minutes on each side, until cooked through. Set aside chicken and keep warm; drain skillet. Add water, juice and bouillon to skillet and simmer until blended; pour over chicken.

Makes 6 servings.

> 12 boneless, skinless
>   chicken tenderloins
> 1/2 t. pepper
> 1/2 t. garlic powder
> 1 egg, beaten
> 2 T. milk
> 1 c. dry bread crumbs
> 1 T. margarine
> 2 T. oil
> 1/2 c. water
> 1/4 c. lemon juice
> 1 t. chicken bouillon
>   granules

KITCHEN TIP

Preserve herbs by placing them
in an ice tray, covering with olive
oil or water and freezing them.
Just pop one out of the tray when
you need it for cooking.

ROSEMARY ROASTED TURKEY

ZOE BENNETT
COLUMBIA, SC

What could be better than the aroma of turkey roasting in the oven?

3/4 c. olive oil
3 T. garlic, minced
2 T. fresh rosemary, chopped
1 T. dried basil
1 T. Italian seasoning
1 t. pepper
salt to taste
12-lb. turkey, thawed if frozen

In a small bowl, combine all ingredients except turkey. Set aside. Using your hands, loosen turkey skin from breast. Work skin loose to the end of the drumstick, being careful not to tear skin. Rub a generous amount of olive oil mixture under skin. Rub remaining mixture over the outside of skin. Use wooden toothpicks to fasten skin over any exposed meat. Place turkey on the rack in a roasting pan; add about 1/4 inch water to bottom of pan. Bake, uncovered, at 325 degrees for 3 to 4 hours, until temperature on a meat thermometer reads 165 degrees when inserted into the breast. Let stand 20 to 30 minutes before carving.

Makes 16 servings.

KITCHEN TIP

Keep reheated food moist in the microwave by placing a cup of water in the microwave with your food.

HOMESTYLE POT ROAST

KAREN CROSBY
MYRTLE BEACH, SC

An absolutely delicious pot roast...and so easy to fix!

Shake flour in a roasting bag; place bag in a 13"x9" baking pan. Add water and soup mix to bag; squeeze bag to combine with flour. Add roast to bag; turn bag to coat roast with flour mixture. Place potatoes, onion and carrots in bag around roast. Close bag with provided nylon tie; cut six, 1/2-inch slits into top of bag. Tuck ends of bag into pan. Bake at 325 degrees for 2 hours, or until roast reaches desired doneness, about 140 to 145 degrees on a meat thermometer for medium. Sprinkle with parsley before serving, if desired.

Serves 6 to 8.

1/4 c. all-purpose flour
2/3 c. water
1-oz. pkg. onion soup mix
3 to 4-lb. beef rump roast
4 redskin potatoes, quartered
1 onion, quartered
16-oz. pkg. baby carrots
Optional: chopped fresh parsley

SWISS ALPS CASEROLE

PAM ENEBRAD
BEAUFORT, SC

I created this recipe to duplicate a dish our family enjoyed while we were living in Switzerland. We lived in a mountain village that specialized in making its own sausage. Family & friends love it!

5 potatoes, peeled and cubed

14-oz. pkg. Kielbasa sausage ring, sliced

1 onion, chopped

Optional: 1 to 2 slices bacon, chopped

1 c. penne pasta, cooked

8-oz. pkg. shredded Gruyère or Swiss cheese

In a large saucepan, cover potatoes with water and boil until tender; drain and set aside. In a skillet over medium-high heat, brown sausage, onion and bacon, if using; drain. Combine all ingredients; transfer to a 13"x9" baking pan that has been sprayed with non-stick vegetable spray. Bake, uncovered, at 350 degrees for 30 minutes, or until cheese is melted.

Serves 4 to 6.

BAKED TURKEY WINGS

MARGARET RICHARDSON
GOOSE CREEK, SC

When I was on a tight budget, this recipe was so inexpensive, yet so tasty. The savory turkey just falls off the bone! Serve with buttered noodles and steamed broccoli for a wonderful meal.

Place wings in an ungreased, aluminum foil-lined 13"x9" baking pan. Top each wing with a pat of butter; sprinkle with seasonings. Cover with aluminum foil. Bake at 350 degrees for 2 hours.

Serves 2 to 4.

4 turkey wings, separated
paprika, salt and pepper to taste
2 T. butter, sliced

MAMA'S MEATLOAF

MAXINE BLAKELY
SENECA, SC

My mother has made this recipe for years. Once you've tried it, you won't want to make any other meatloaf! The glaze is what makes the meatloaf so delicious.

In a large bowl, mix together beef, eggs, milk, cracker crumbs, salt, pepper and onion, if using. Form into a loaf and place in an ungreased 9"x5" loaf pan. Bake, covered, at 350 degrees for 45 minutes. Mix remaining ingredients; spread over meatloaf. Bake, uncovered, an additional 15 minutes.

Serves 6 to 8.

1-1/2 lbs. ground beef
2 eggs, beaten
3/4 c. milk
2/3 c. saltine cracker crumbs
salt and pepper to taste
Optional: 2 t. onion, chopped
1/4 c. catsup
2 t. brown sugar, packed
1 t. mustard
1 T. lemon juice

BEEF TIPS & GRAVY

**SUSAN ICE
SIMPSONVILLE, SC**

The house smells sooo good when this is cooking...the tender beef just melts in your mouth. A real warmer-upper for chilly weather!

1 c. all-purpose flour
1 t. onion powder
1 t. garlic powder
salt and pepper to taste
2-1/2 lbs. beef tips or
  stew beef, cubed
2 to 3 T. oil
1 c. water
.87-oz. pkg. brown gravy
  mix
1/4 c. Worcestershire
  sauce
1/4 c. soy sauce
mashed potatoes or
  cooked egg noodles

Mix flour and seasonings in a large plastic zipping bag. Add beef; shake to coat beef thoroughly. Pour oil into a large heavy skillet and heat over medium-high heat for 2 to 3 minutes. Add beef to skillet; brown on all sides. Blend water, gravy mix and sauces in a slow cooker; add beef. Cover and cook on low setting for 6 to 8 hours, or on high setting for 4 to 5 hours. Add a little water if needed to thin gravy mixture. Serve over mashed potatoes or cooked noodles.

Serves 4 to 6.

SLOW-COOKER MEXICAN BEEF

JOANN
GOOSEBERRY PATCH

This easy barbacoa-style beef is perfect for burritos, bowls and tacos!

Spray a slow cooker with non-stick vegetable spray. Blend vinegar, beef broth and seasoning together. Place roast in slow-cooker and pour broth mixture overtop. Cover and cook on low setting for 8 hours. Shred beef and serve.

Serves 6.

1/3 c. apple cider vinegar
1/2 c. beef broth
2 1-oz. pkg's. taco seasoning
3 1/2 lb. boneless chuck roast, fat trimmed

SAUCY BBQ PORK TENDERLOIN

GINA FILIPPELLI
TAYLORS, SC

My son and I came up with this recipe together...it's tasty served on rolls or enjoyed all by itself. Just add French fries or crispy golden potato puffs for a meal everyone will love.

Place pork in a slow cooker; season with salt and pepper. Pour water over pork. Cover and cook on high setting for about 5 hours. Pour off half of remaining liquid in slow cooker; add 3/4 of barbecue sauce. Cover and cook on high setting for one additional hour. Reduce setting to low; cook for one additional hour, or until pork is very tender and falls apart. Serve on Kaiser rolls, if desired, accompanied by remaining barbecue sauce.

Serves 4 to 6.

2 to 3-lb. pork tenderloin, trimmed
salt and pepper to taste
3 c. water
18-oz. bottle barbecue sauce, divided
Optional: 12-oz. pkg. Kaiser rolls, split

TURKEY SCALLOP

BETHANNA KORTIE
GREER, SC

I inherited my husband's mother's cookbook, filled with old-fashioned handwritten recipes from his mother, grandmother and great-grandmother! I adapted this dish from one grandmotherly recipe. It's a wonderful way to enjoy holiday leftovers.

2-1/2 c. seasoned croutons
1/2 c. butter, melted and divided
1 c. celery, diced
1/2 c. chicken broth
1-1/2 c. milk
1/4 c. all-purpose flour
1 c. roast turkey, diced
Garnish: fresh parsley

In a bowl, drizzle croutons with 1/4 cup melted butter; toss to coat and set aside. In a saucepan over medium heat, cook celery in broth until tender. Drain; pour broth into a 2-cup glass measuring cup. Add enough milk to broth to make 2 cups. In the same saucepan, stir flour into remaining melted butter. Gradually add reserved broth mixture. Cook until thickened, stirring constantly. Arrange half of croutons in an ungreased 1-1/2 quart casserole dish. Top with turkey, celery and remaining croutons; pour sauce over top. Bake, uncovered, at 350 degrees until heated through, 20 to 25 minutes. Garnish with parsley.

Makes 4 servings.

ONE-DISH TOMATO PORK DINNER

ROBIN LANGLEY
LAKE CITY, SC

One of my family's favorite dinners! Just add a crisp salad and fresh-baked bread, and you are sure to have a wonderful meal.

Place tenderloin in a large slow cooker, fat-side up. Pour all tomatoes with their juice over tenderloin. Add vegetables; gently stir in. Cover and cook on low setting for 6 to 8 hours. About 30 minutes before serving time, add rice, stirring into liquid in slow cooker. Cover and cook for another 30 minutes. Slice tenderloin; serve with vegetables and rice from slow cooker.

Serves 8.

4-lb. pork tenderloin

15-oz. can tomato sauce

15-oz. can diced tomatoes

15-oz. can stewed tomatoes

6-oz. tomato paste

1 green pepper, sliced

1 yellow onion, diced

2 potatoes, peeled and sliced

8-oz. pkg. baby carrots, sliced

1 c. instant rice, uncooked

salt and pepper to taste

BEEF & SHELL STUFF

**LESLIE HARVIE
SIMPSONVILLE, SC**

I found the original recipe for this dish written in the back of one of my mom's cookbooks. It quickly became one of my teenage son Tyler's favorite meals. When asked what we should have for dinner, he often answers, "Beef & Shell Stuff!" Sometimes I double the recipe... teenage boys can eat a lot!

1 onion, chopped
3 cloves garlic, minced
1 T. olive oil
1 lb. ground beef
2 14-1/2 oz. cans stewed
   tomatoes
8-oz. pkg. shell
   macaroni, uncooked
1-3/4 c. water
1 t. Italian seasoning
salt and pepper to taste
Optional: grated
   Parmesan cheese

In a large skillet over medium heat, sauté onion and garlic in olive oil until translucent; drain. Add beef and cook until browned; drain. Stir in tomatoes with juice and uncooked macaroni. Pour water over beef mixture; stir in seasonings. Bring to a boil. Reduce heat to low. Cover and simmer until macaroni is tender and liquid is absorbed, about 10 minutes. Sprinkle individual servings with Parmesan cheese, if desired.

Makes 6 servings.

JUST FOR FUN

South Carolina produces the most peaches on the east side of the Mississippi and second-most in the entire US, behind California, making it the official state fruit.

WINTER STEAK KABOBS

GLENDA TOLBERT
MOORE, SC

Toss everything in the slow cooker before you head out for your holiday shopping. Serve with a tossed salad and garlic bread when you get back! Who needs a grill?

Place steak and potatoes in a slow cooker; sprinkle with salt and pepper. Add pepper, onion and pineapple; cover with barbecue sauce. Cover and cook on low setting for 6 hours, or high setting for 4 hours, until steak and vegetables are tender.

Serves 2 to 4.

1-lb. beef sirloin tip steak, cubed
2 14-1/2 oz. cans whole potatoes, drained
salt and pepper to taste
1 green pepper, sliced
1 onion, sliced
15-1/4 oz. can pineapple chunks, drained
18-oz. bottle barbecue sauce

DILL BEEF NOODLES

PAIGE BEAR
LYMAN, SC

This is a favorite of our little girls. It's easy to prepare in a slow cooker. The gravy is delicious over the noodles...we love to sop it up with bread!

Brown beef in a skillet over medium heat; add onion and cook until tender. Drain; stir in garlic and cook for 30 seconds. Transfer beef mixture to a 3-quart slow cooker. Add beef broth, Worcestershire sauce and seasonings. Cover and cook on low setting for 6 to 8 hours, or on high setting for 4 hours. In a cup, stir together cornstarch and water. Stir into mixture in slow cooker; cover and turn to high setting for 30 minutes. Serve beef mixture over cooked noodles.

Makes 6 servings.

1 lb. ground beef
3/4 c. onion
1 clove garlic, minced
2 14-oz. cans beef broth
3 T. Worcestershire sauce
1/4 t. dried dill weed
1/4 t. dried thyme
1/4 t. kosher salt
2 T. cornstarch
2 T. cold water
cooked egg noodles

CHINESE SOY CHICKEN WINGS

ZOE BENNETT
COLUMBIA, SC

My family loves these spicy, sticky wings. Serve with steamed rice and a steamed veggie for dinner, or let them steal the show at your next party. Pass the napkins, please!

1/3 c. chicken broth

1/3 c. sherry or chicken broth

1/3 c. soy sauce

2 t. fresh ginger, peeled and grated

2 t. Dijon mustard

1 clove garlic, pressed

1/4 t. red pepper flakes

24 chicken wings, separated

1/4 c. apricot jam

1 T. cornstarch

1 T. cold water

In a large container, combine all ingredients except chicken wings, jam, cornstarch and water. Add wings to bowl; toss to coat evenly. Cover and refrigerate for 2 hours to overnight, stirring twice. Transfer wings to a 6-quart electric pressure cooker. Pour marinade into a small saucepan; bring to a boil and pour over wings. Close and lock lid; set heat to high. When pressure cooker reaches high pressure, turn down heat as low as possible. Set timer and cook for 14 minutes; turn off. Let stand for 5 minutes. Open pressure cooker using quick release method. Transfer wings to a platter; set aside. Stir jam into liquid in pot; whisk until melted. Stir together cornstarch and cold water in a cup; add to pot and stir well. Return wings to pot; stir gently to coat evenly. Simmer for 2 minutes, or until sauce is thickened and translucent. Transfer wings to a serving plate, using tongs.

Makes about 2 dozen.

GARDEN MINI MEATLOAVES

BETHANNA KORTIE
GREER, SC

A terrific way to sneak in veggies for picky eaters! I love to serve buttery mashed potatoes and green beans with these meatloaves.

In a large bowl, combine 1/2 cup bread crumbs and remaining ingredients except cheese; mix well. Divide mixture among 6 ungreased ramekins; sprinkle evenly with remaining bread crumbs. Set ramekins on a baking sheet. Bake, uncovered, at 400 degrees for 30 minutes. Using a turkey baster, drain off drippings. Sprinkle meatloaves evenly with cheese. Bake an additional 5 minutes, until cheese melts.

Serves 6.

1 c. dry bread crumbs, divided
1-1/2 lbs. ground beef
1 egg, beaten
2 T. Worcestershire sauce
1 c. green, red or yellow pepper, grated
1/2 zucchini, grated
1/2 sweet onion, chopped
1 T. fresh thyme, minced
3 leaves fresh basil, minced
salt and pepper to taste
1 c. shredded Colby Jack cheese

MYRTLE BEACH CORN DODGERS

**TONI CURRIN
DILLON, SC**

*These hush puppy-like morsels are good with fried fish or alongside a
bowl of chili.*

2 eggs, beaten
1-1/2 c. milk
2 c. cornmeal
1 c. all-purpose flour
1 T. baking powder
1/2 t. salt
oil for deep frying

In a bowl, whisk together eggs and milk; set aside. In a large bowl, combine remaining ingredients; stir in egg mixture. In a deep fryer, heat several inches oil to 350 degrees. Working in batches, drop batter into oil by spoonfuls. Cook until golden on all sides.

Makes 6 to 8 servings.

PRESENTATION

Placing a lemon or lime wedge on the edge of a salad plate offers your guests an optional spritz of flavor and makes the salad look fresh and pretty too!

MEXICAN STIR-FRIED RICE

JOHN NEWSOME
COLUMBIA, SC

This is definitely a family favorite, created one day from what we could find in our pantry! Now we come back to this recipe time & time again because it is delicious and budget-friendly.

Cook rice according to package directions; drain and rinse. Spread rice on a large plate and place in refrigerator to cool. Heat oil over medium- high heat in a large skillet. Add chicken; shred with a fork and stir until warmed through. Add garlic; sauté for 30 seconds. Stir in beans; heat through. Stir in sweet potato and tomato; add cooked rice. Cook, stirring constantly and scraping bottom of skillet until well mixed. If necessary, add a little more oil to keep rice from sticking. Stir in salsa and chili powder.

Makes 6 to 8 servings.

- 1-1/2 c. long-cooking brown rice, uncooked
- 3 T. olive oil
- 10-oz. can chicken breast, drained
- 2 cloves garlic, minced
- 15-oz. can black beans, drained and rinsed
- 1 sweet potato, peeled and diced
- 1 tomato, diced
- 3 to 4 T. favorite salsa
- 2 t. chili powder, or more to taste

BROCCOLI-CHICKEN LASAGNA

MONICA WILKINSON
BURTON, SC

A tasty twist on a familiar dish...the kids will love it!

1/4 c. butter
1/4 c. all-purpose flour
1 T. chicken bouillon granules
pepper to taste
1/2 t. Italian seasoning
2 c. milk
2 c. shredded Italian-blend cheese
2 c. broccoli flowerets, cooked
1 c. cooked chicken, diced
4 strips cooked lasagna, divided

Melt butter in a saucepan over medium-low heat; stir in flour, bouillon, pepper and Italian seasoning. Gradually stir in milk; cook and stir until thickened. Add cheese; stir until melted. Mix in broccoli and chicken. Spread 1/2 cup mixture in the bottom of an 8"x8" baking pan sprayed with non-stick vegetable spray. Top with half of lasagna. Top with half of remaining sauce; repeat layers. Bake, uncovered, at 350 degrees for 30 to 40 minutes.

Serves 4 to 6.

KITCHEN TIP

Scrub cast-iron skillets with salt instead of dish soap to keep them clean and rust-free.

SIMPLY SCRUMPTIOUS STICKY WINGS

DEBRA JOHNSON
MYRTLE BEACH, SC

Get out the napkins, because these delectable treats are as messy as they are tasty. The ginger really adds a nice zip to the sauce...we love to have a big plate of these on game days.

Combine 1/4 cup brown sugar, one tablespoon soy sauce, garlic, ginger and 1/4 teaspoon cayenne pepper in a slow cooker. Season chicken wings with salt and pepper; add to sugar mixture. Toss wings to coat well. Cover and cook on low setting for 4 to 5 hours, until chicken is tender and no longer pink in the center. Remove wings to a rack on an aluminum foil-lined baking sheet; set aside. In a bowl, combine remaining brown sugar, soy sauce and cayenne pepper, water and tomato paste; mix well. Brush wings with half of sauce. Broil wings until crisp on one side, about 10 minutes. Turn wings and brush with remaining sauce; broil until other side is crisp, about 5 minutes.

3/4 c. dark brown sugar, packed and divided
1/4 c. soy sauce, divided
4 cloves garlic, minced
2 T. fresh ginger, minced
1/2 t. cayenne pepper, divided
4 lbs. chicken wings
salt and pepper to taste
1/4 c. water
1/4 c. tomato paste

Makes 8 servings.

SHORT RIBS & GRAVY

**DALE DRIGGERS
LEXINGTON, SC**

This is the best short rib recipe I know. The meat just falls off the bone, and the gravy is delicious...serve over rice, polenta, pasta or mashed potatoes.

2-1/2 lbs. beef short ribs
salt and pepper to taste
1 T. olive oil
2 carrots, peeled and chopped
2 stalks celery, chopped
3 cloves garlic, chopped
1/3 c. balsamic vinegar
1/3 c. red wine or beef broth
1/3 c. crushed tomatoes
3 bay leaves

Season ribs on all sides with salt and pepper. Heat oil in a large skillet over medium heat. Brown ribs on all sides in oil; drain and set aside. Arrange carrots and celery in a slow cooker. Add remaining ingredients to carrot mixture. Nestle ribs into mixture in slow cooker. Cover and cook on low setting for 8 to 9 hours. Remove ribs; discard bay leaves. Mash or blend vegetable mixture to desired consistency. Serve ribs drizzled with gravy from slow cooker.

Serves 6 to 8.

SAUCY RIBS

**ZOE BENNETT
COLUMBIA, SC**

Better make plenty...these will disappear quickly!

1 t. dry mustard
1/2 t. allspice
1 t. salt
1 t. pepper
3 lbs. baby back pork ribs, sliced into 4-inch pieces
1/2 c. water
1-1/2 c. barbecue sauce

Combine all seasonings in a small bowl; rub onto ribs. Place in a slow cooker and pour water over top. Cover and cook on low setting for 8 to 9 hours, until ribs are tender when pierced with a fork. Remove ribs from slow cooker; discard cooking liquid. Replace ribs in slow cooker and add barbecue sauce. Cover and cook on low setting for one additional hour.

Makes 6 servings.

SLOW-COOKER PORK RIB RAGU

**JOANN
GOOSEBERRY PATCH**

My family loves this hearty dish...it's simple to make, so I'm happy to make it for them. Sometimes we have it as our lucky pork dish on New Year's Day.

Add carrots, celery, onion and garlic to a 6-quart slow cooker. Place pork ribs on top, overlapping as necessary. In a bowl, stir together tomato sauce, beef broth, vinegar and seasonings; spoon over pork. Cover and cook on low setting for 6 to 8 hours, until pork is tender. With slotted spoon, remove pork to a platter; cool slightly. Shred pork and set aside, discarding bones. In a small cup, whisk together flour and water until smooth. Skim fat from sauce in slow cooker; stir in flour mixture. Turn slow cooker to high setting. Cook, uncovered, about 15 minutes. Stir in pork; cook another 5 minutes, or until heated through. To serve, ladle pork and sauce over noodles.

Makes 8 to 10 servings.

2 carrots, peeled and coarsely chopped

2 stalks celery, coarsely chopped

1 onion, thinly sliced

1 clove garlic, minced

4 lbs. meaty pork spareribs, cut into serving-size pieces

15-oz. can tomato sauce

1/2 c. beef broth

1-1/2 T. balsamic vinegar

1/2 t. dried oregano

1/2 t. dried thyme

1/2 t. salt

2 T. all-purpose flour

1/4 c. cold water

cooked egg noodles

SLOW-COOKER BALSAMIC CHICKEN

LESLIE HARVIE
SIMPSONVILLE, SC

Tender slow-cooked chicken and savory fresh herbs make this dish a winner. It's nice to come home to a delicious, healthy meal after a long day at work or play.

4 boneless, skinless chicken breasts

1 onion, thinly sliced

4 cloves garlic, finely chopped

2 t. fresh oregano, chopped

2 t. fresh basil, chopped

1/2 t. fresh thyme, chopped

1/2 t. salt

1/2 t. pepper

1/2 c. balsamic vinegar

28-oz. can fire-roasted diced tomatoes

Spray a 4-quart slow cooker with non-stick vegetable spray. Arrange chicken breasts in crock; top with onion slices. Sprinkle with garlic, herbs, salt and pepper; drizzle with balsamic vinegar. Spoon undrained tomatoes over all. Cover and cook on low setting for 7 to 8 hours, until chicken juices run clear.

Makes 6 servings.

NO-BAKE HAM PIZZA

ZOE BENNETT
COLUMBIA, SC

Sprinkle on some diced carrot and chopped broccoli too...the kids will love eating their veggies!

Combine cream cheese, mayonnaise and horseradish sauce in a small bowl; blend well. Spread over pizza crust. Top with ham, tomatoes and lettuce; drizzle with salad dressing. Cut into wedges and serve immediately.

Serves 6.

1/2 c. cream cheese with chives, softened

1/4 c. mayonnaise

2 T. horseradish sauce

1 Italian pizza crust

1-1/2 c. cooked ham, chopped

1-1/2 c. roma tomatoes, chopped

1/2 c. lettuce, shredded

1/4 c. creamy Italian salad dressing

SMOKY MOUNTAIN BARBECUE SAUCE

TONI CURRIN
DILLON, SC

Great on chicken...just add corn on the cob and your meal is complete!

Heat oil in a skillet over medium heat; add onion and garlic. Cook until onion is clear. Add remaining ingredients; simmer until sauce has thickened.

Makes about 2-1/2 cups.

1/4 c. oil

1/2 c. onion, chopped

1 clove garlic, minced

1 c. tomato purée

1 c. water

1 bay leaf, crushed

3 whole cloves

1 T. chili powder

1/4 c. brown sugar, packed

1/4 c. cider vinegar

CHICKEN LASAGNA WITH ROASTED RED PEPPER SAUCE

**KAREN SMITH
ROCK HILL, SC**

This recipe reminds me of home every time I make it.

4 c. cooked chicken, finely chopped

2 8-oz. containers chive-and-onion cream cheese

10-oz. pkg. frozen chopped spinach, thawed and well drained

1 t. seasoned pepper

3/4 t. garlic salt

9 no-boil lasagna noodles, uncooked

2 c. shredded Italian 3-cheese blend

ROASTED RED PEPPER SAUCE:

16-oz. jar creamy Alfredo sauce

12-oz. jar roasted red peppers, drained

3/4 c. grated Parmesan cheese

1/2 t. red pepper flakes

Stir together chicken, cream cheese, spinach, pepper and salt. Layer a lightly greased 11"x7" baking pan with one-third of Roasted Red Pepper Sauce, 3 noodles, one-third of chicken mixture and one-third of cheese. Repeat layers twice. Place baking pan on a baking sheet. Bake, covered, at 350 degrees for 50 to 55 minutes, until hot and bubbly. Uncover and bake 15 more minutes.

Serves 6 to 8.

Roasted Red Pepper Sauce:
Process all ingredients in a food processor until smooth, stopping to scrape down sides.

ZESTY CREOLE BAKE

**DEBRA JOHNSON
MYRTLE BEACH, SC**

This recipe is good when you're in the mood for something a little tangy!

Combine boiling water and rice; cover and set aside. Meanwhile, melt butter in a skillet over medium heat. Add onion and garlic; cook until tender, about 4 minutes. Add celery and green pepper; cook for about 3 minutes, until tender but not browned. Add flour and stir well; cook for 3 more minutes. Stir in milk and bring just to a boil. Stir in chili sauce, hot sauce, salt and pepper. Place rice in a greased 13"x9" baking pan. Arrange fish fillets over rice in a single layer. Place sliced tomatoes over fish; pour sauce over top. Bake, uncovered, at 400 degrees for 20 minutes, or until fish flakes easily with fork.

Serves 4.

3 c. boiling water
1-1/2 c. instant rice, uncooked
1/4 c. butter
1 onion, chopped
1 clove garlic, minced
2 stalks celery, chopped
1 green pepper, chopped
1/4 c. all-purpose flour
2 c. milk
1/2 c. chili sauce
1/2 t. hot pepper sauce
1 t. salt
1/4 t. pepper
1 lb. cod fillets, thawed if frozen
2 tomatoes, sliced

CHAPTER FIVE

ATLANTIC COAST

Appetizers & Snacks

WHETHER YOU ARE HAVING
COMPANY OR JUST NEED A
LITTLE SNACK TO HOLD YOU OVER
UNTIL THE NEXT MEAL, YOU'LL
FIND THESE RECIPES ARE GREAT
FOR TAKING ON-THE-GO OR AS A
FAVORITE APPETIZER.

YANKEE ICED TEA

JULIE HARRIS
BOILING SPRINGS, SC

Growing up in the Pennsylvania countryside, I remember my mom making this tea for my dad every evening to go alongside one of her hearty homemade dinners. Following in my mom's footsteps, I now make this often for my own husband. Add a full cup of sugar if you like your tea sweeter.

2 c. boiling water
6 tea bags
1/8 t. baking soda
3/4 c. sugar
6 c. cold water
Garnish: ice cubes,
  lemon wedges

In a one-gallon pitcher, combine boiling water and tea bags. Cover; let stand for 15 to 20 minutes to steep. Remove tea bags. Stir in baking soda and sugar until dissolved. Add cold water; cover and refrigerate. Serve over ice cubes with a squeeze of lemon.

Makes 4 to 6 servings.

PRESENTATION

Use a mini cookie cutter to cut the center out of cucumber slices. Then cut the same shape from a block of cheese. Place the cheese cut-outs inside the cucumber.

TANGY RADISH BITES

**KAREN SMITH
ROCK HILL, SC**

These beautiful little finger sandwiches will be the talk of the party. My friends just love them!

Mix butter, chives, sesame seed, ginger and oil in a bowl. Add salt and pepper and mix well. Spread mixture over one side of each baguette slice. Top with radishes, overlapping slightly. Garnish as desired.

Makes 16 servings.

2 T. butter, softened

3 T. fresh chives, chopped

1 T. toasted sesame seed

3/4 t. fresh ginger, peeled and grated

1/4 t. sesame oil

1/8 t. salt

1/8 t. pepper

1 whole-grain baguette, sliced 1/4-inch thick

10 radishes, thinly sliced

Garnish: edible flowers, pea sprouts

SMOKED PIMENTO CHEESE DIP

MARY BETTUCHY
COLUMBIA, SC

We're a military family, so we've been stationed all over the country and get to try different regional foods. Here in South Carolina, one of the most delicious things I've discovered is pimento cheese! The smoky flavor is my own spin on this classic.

8-oz. pkg. smoked Cheddar cheese, shredded

8-oz. pkg. cream cheese, softened

2 4-oz. jars pimentos or roasted red peppers, drained and diced

1/4 c. mayonnaise

1/2 t. smoked salt or 1/4 t. smoke-flavored cooking sauce

1/4 t. hot pepper sauce

1/4 t. red pepper flakes

pita chips

In a food processor or blender, combine all ingredients except pita chips. Pulse until combined. If mixture is too thick, add a little more mayonnaise. If more smoky flavor or heat is desired, add more smoke or hot sauce to taste. Serve with pita chips.

Serves 8.

CHEDDAR FONDUE

KRISTY MARKNERS
FORT MILL, SC

*We love making fondue and serving it with a variety of dippers. It's a
fun appetizer to serve at parties!*

In a bowl, toss cheeses with flour; set aside. In a
saucepan over medium heat, bring beer or broth to
a slow boil. Reduce heat to a simmer. Slowly stir in
cheese mixture, stirring constantly. When cheese is
fully melted, stir in Worcestershire sauce, mustard
and hot sauce. Transfer to a warmed fondue pot.
Serve with dippers.

Serves 8.

2-1/2 c. shredded extra-
sharp Cheddar cheese

1-1/2 c. shredded Swiss
cheese

1 T. all-purpose flour

12-oz. bottle beer or
1-1/2 c. broth

1/2 t. Worcestershire
sauce

1/2 t. dry mustard

hot pepper sauce to
taste

variety of dippers, such
as bread cubes, lightly
steamed veggies or
apple slices

JUST FOR FUN

The world's smallest police station is in
Ridgeway. It's about as big as a toll booth
and was in full use from 1940-1990. The
new, upgraded post office is right beside it.

SPICY CHEESE SHORTBREAD

ZOE BENNETT
COLUMBIA, SC

These crisp homemade crackers are delicious all by themselves...even better with your favorite spreads.

8-oz. pkg. shredded
  sharp Cheddar cheese
1-1/2 c. all-purpose flour
3/4 t. dry mustard
1/4 t. cayenne pepper
1/2 c. butter, melted
Optional: 1 T. water

In a large bowl, toss together cheese, flour, mustard and pepper; stir in butter. Knead until dough forms; add water if dough feels dry. Divide into 2 balls. On a floured surface, roll out each ball 1/4-inch thick. Cut out with desired cookie cutters. Place on ungreased baking sheets. Bake at 375 degrees for 10 to 12 minutes, until lightly golden. Cool on a wire rack.

Makes about 3 dozen.

SWEET & TANGY CORN & BLACK BEAN SALSA

LESLIE HARVIE
SIMPSONVILLE, SC

My cousin gave me this recipe a couple of years ago, and I have made it for every party and holiday gathering ever since. I usually double the recipe because everyone loves it so much!

1-1/2 c. frozen corn,
  thawed and drained
15-1/2 oz. can black
  beans, drained and
  rinsed
3 green onions, chopped
1 red pepper, diced
2 T. sugar
1/4 c. cider vinegar
1/4 c. olive oil
tortilla chips

In a large bowl, stir together corn, beans, onions and pepper. Add sugar, vinegar and oil; stir well to combine. Cover and refrigerate at least one hour before serving. Serve with tortilla chips.

Makes 6 to 8 servings.

RANCH-STUFFED MUSHROOMS

**MANDY MEARS
LEXINGTON, SC**

This is my tried & true recipe whenever I need an appetizer for a gathering. Sometimes people are standing by to gobble them up as they come out of the oven!

In a large bowl, mix together cheeses, mayonnaise, dressing mix, onion and parsley until well blended. Spread stuffing out on a plate. Fill mushroom caps with cream cheese mixture, then press the tops into the stuffing so that a generous amount of stuffing crumbs sticks to cream cheese mixture. Place mushrooms on an aluminum foil-lined baking sheet. Drizzle melted butter over mushrooms. Bake at 375 degrees for about 30 minutes, until hot and bubbly. Cool slightly before serving.

Makes 2 dozen.

8-oz. pkg. cream cheese, softened
1/4 c. grated Parmesan cheese
1/4 c. mayonnaise
1-1/2 T. ranch salad dressing mix
1 T. onion, minced
2 t. dried parsley
6-oz. pkg. chicken-flavored stuffing mix
1-1/2 lbs. whole mushrooms, stems removed and discarded
1/2 c. butter, melted

JUST FOR FUN

The Angel Oak in Charleston is estimated to be more than 400-500 years old. The tree currently has a circumference of 25 feet, a diameter spread of 160 feet and covers about 17,100 square feet of ground.

PICKLED FRANKS & CAULIFLOWER

NANCY KAISER
YORK, SC

My sweet mother-in-law shared a lot of good recipes with me over the years, and this one stands out as a favorite of mine. She always kept a jar of this in the fridge during the holidays. It's great for a finger food, evening snack or for lunch. This keeps in the fridge for a couple of weeks, so it will be ready anytime you are.

1 cauliflower, cut into
   bite-size flowerets
3 lbs. frankfurters, cut
   into 1-inch pieces
1 onion, sliced and
   separated into rings
3 c. water
2-1/4 c. white vinegar
1/2 c. sugar
1 T. mixed pickling
   spices
1 t. salt
1/2 t. red pepper flakes

Cover cauliflower with water. Bring to a boil over medium-high heat and cook to tender-crisp; drain well. In a one-gallon jar, layer cauliflower, franks and onion rings; set aside. Combine remaining ingredients in a saucepan. Bring to a boil over high heat, stirring until sugar dissolves. Pour over ingredients in jar. Cool; add lid and refrigerate at least one day before serving. May keep refrigerated for 2 weeks.

Makes one gallon.

AUTUMN APPLE DIP

LESLIE HARVIE
SIMPSONVILLE, SC

My kids and I enjoy snacking on this sweet dip while we carve our Halloween pumpkins.

8-oz. pkg. cream cheese,
   softened
3/4 c. brown sugar,
   packed
1 t. vanilla extract
1 c. chopped peanuts
apple slices

In a bowl, combine all ingredients except apples; mix well. Cover and chill until serving time. Serve with apple slices.

Serves 16.

MINI BAJA SHRIMP TACOS

**KAREN SMITH
ROCK HILL, SC**

*I like to serve these with a decorative toothpick going through the tops
of the tortillas to hold them together and make them easy to pick up.*

Chop shrimp, discarding tails. Heat oil in a large skillet over medium-high heat. Add shrimp to the skillet and sauté for 2 to 3 minutes on each side, until pink and cooked through. In a separate bowl, mix mayonnaise with remaining ingredients, except garnish. Combine shrimp with mayonnaise mixture. Toss to coat. Spoon shrimp mixture into each tortilla, top with garnish and serve.

Makes about 10.

- 1 lbs. shrimp, peeled and cleaned
- 1 T. vegetable oil
- 1/2 c. mayonnaise
- 1 T. lime juice
- 1/2 t. sea salt
- 1 t. garlic, minced
- 1/4 c. red onion, finely diced
- 1/4 t. ground cumin
- 1/4 t. cayenne pepper
- 1/4 t. pepper
- 10 4-inch white corn tortillas
- Garnish: finely shredded cabbage, Cotija cheese, diced avocado

SLOW-COOKED BRIE

**ZOE BENNETT
COLUMBIA, SC**

*A scrumptious snack with no effort at all! Serve with apple slices and
toasted baguette slices.*

Trim and discard rind from top of cheese; place cheese in a small slow cooker. Top with cranberries and pecans. Cover and cook on slow setting for 3 to 4 hours, or on high setting for 2 hours, until cheese is very soft. Serve warm.

Makes 8 servings.

- 8-oz. pkg. round brie cheese, unwrapped
- 1/3 c. candied or toasted pecans, chopped
- 1/4 c. sweetened dried cranberries, chopped

MUSHROOM-CHEESE PINWHEELS

MARY BETTUCHY
COLUMBIA, SC

I make these every year for Thanksgiving...they must be on the table! My sister Sarah loves them so much she makes them every year too. She lives across the country from me, so we don't often get to celebrate the holidays together. This recipe joins us together on Thanksgiving, as we both have it on our tables! They are even good eaten cold right out of the fridge.

2 T. butter

1/2 lb. mushrooms, very finely minced

2 cloves garlic, minced

1 shallot, minced

1 t. dried thyme

1/2 c. red wine or beef broth

salt and pepper to taste

1 sheet frozen puff pastry dough, thawed

4-oz. container spreadable cheese with garlic & fine herbs, softened

Melt butter in a large skillet over medium heat. Add mushrooms, garlic, shallot and thyme. Sauté for about 5 minutes, until vegetables are soft and starting to turn golden. Add wine or broth. Over low heat, simmer until liquid has almost completely evaporated, stirring occasionally, about 10 minutes. Remove from heat. Season with salt and pepper; set aside. On a lightly floured surface, gently roll out puff pastry to 1/8-inch thick. Spread cheese over pastry, leaving a 1/2-inch border on all 4 sides. Spread mushroom mixture over cheese layer. Roll up pastry jelly-roll style, pinching seam to seal well. Slice into rounds 3/4-inch thick. Place on a parchment paper-lined baking sheet. Bake at 375 degrees for about 20 minutes, until puffed and golden. Serve warm.

Makes 4 servings.

KRISTY'S ZUCCHINI STICKS

**KRISTY MARKNERS
FORT MILL, SC**

*I've taste-tested fried zucchini sticks at a restaurant. These are much
healthier for you and taste better too!*

Beat egg whites in a shallow bowl until foamy.
Combine bread crumbs and seasonings in a
separate shallow bowl. Toss zucchini strips in egg
whites, then in bread crumbs to coat. Place on a
baking sheet coated with non-stick vegetable spray.
Sprinkle with Parmesan cheese; spray tops lightly
with non-stick spray. Bake at 450 degrees for 15 to
20 minutes, until crisp and golden.

Serves 6.

> 2 egg whites
> 1 c. Italian-flavored
>   panko bread crumbs
> 1/4 t. cayenne pepper
> 1/4 t. seafood seasoning
> 1/4 t. salt
> 1 to 2 zucchini, cut into
>   1/4-inch strips
> Garnish: grated
>   Parmesan cheese

SASSY SHRIMP
COCKTAIL DIP

**JESI ALLEN
CLOVER, SC**

*This dip brings back many fond memories of holidays spent with
friends during winter break from school. We'd make a batch to
snack on while we watched all the classic Christmas movies.*

In a bowl, blend cream cheese and sour cream.
Spread in the bottom of a 9" pie plate or serving
dish. In another bowl, combine catsup, horseradish
and lemon juice. Mix well and spread over cream
cheese mixture. Spread shrimp over catsup mixture.
Cover and chill at least one hour. Serve with
crackers or baguette slices.

Serves 6.

> 2 8-oz. pkgs. cream
>   cheese, softened
> 8-oz. container sour
>   cream
> 1-1/2 c. catsup
> 2 T. prepared
>   horseradish
> 1 T. lemon juice
> 2 4-1/4 oz. cans baby
>   shrimp, drained and
>   coarsely chopped
> snack crackers or
>   baguette slices

SPICED PINEAPPLE PICKS

**LAURIE RUPSIS
AIKEN, SC**

*I got this recipe from my mother and I love it! It is just a little bit
different...a real treat at potlucks and parties.*

20-oz. can pineapple
  chunks
8-oz. can pineapple
  chunks
1-1/4 c. sugar
1/2 c. cider vinegar
4-inch cinnamon stick
8 whole cloves

In a saucepan, combine juice from both cans of
pineapple chunks. Add sugar, vinegar and spices;
bring to a boil over medium heat. Reduce heat to
medium-low. Cover and simmer for 10 minutes. Add
pineapple chunks; return to a boil. Cook, stirring
constantly, until heated through. Serve pineapple
chunks with toothpicks.

Makes 12 servings.

BOILED SHRIMP IN BEER

**KAREN SMITH
ROCK HILL, SC**

*Treat yourself to these super-easy peel & eat shrimp...even
clean-up is a snap! Dump shrimp onto a picnic table covered with
newspaper, then after dinner, just toss the paper, shells and all.*

1 qt. water
12-oz. can regular or
  non-alcoholic beer
1 lemon, sliced
1 onion, chopped
1 stalk celery, diced
1 T. seafood seasoning
2 bay leaves
hot pepper sauce to
  taste
1 lb. uncooked large
  shrimp, cleaned
Garnish: cocktail sauce

Combine all ingredients except shrimp and garnish
in a Dutch oven. Bring to a boil over medium-high
heat. Add shrimp; cover and return to a full boil for
3 to 4 minutes. Stir; remove from heat. Let stand 3
to 4 additional minutes, until shrimp turn pink. Drain
well; discard bay leaves. Serve with cocktail sauce.

Serves 4.

SHERRIED SHRIMP SANDWICHES

DEBRA JOHNSON
MYRTLE BEACH, SC

These little gems are a party favorite in our family!

Cook shrimp using seafood boil according to package directions; drain. Peel shrimp and devein, if desired. Chop shrimp. Stir together shrimp and remaining ingredients except bread and garnish. Spread about one tablespoon filling on half of bread slices. Top each with another bread slice. Cut sandwiches in half diagonally. Garnish, if desired. Store sandwiches covered with a damp paper towel in an airtight container in refrigerator.

Makes about 4 dozen.

1-1/2 lbs. uncooked small shrimp
3-oz. pkg. shrimp, crawfish and crab boil
4-oz. pkg. crumbled blue cheese, softened
1/2 c. cream cheese, softened
Optional: 1/4 c. sherry
5 green onions, minced
1/2 c. celery, diced
1/2 c. walnuts, finely chopped and toasted
1/2 t. seasoned salt
1/4 t. cayenne pepper
3 12-oz. pkgs. party pumpernickel bread
Garnish: fresh dill sprigs

HOMEMADE SOFT PRETZELS

**DEBRA JOHNSON
MYRTLE BEACH, SC**

*Making pretzels with your kids or grandkids is so much fun! Then enjoy
your creations for snacking or alongside a steamy bowl of soup instead
of a hot roll.*

1 env. active dry yeast
1-1/2 c. warm water
1 T. sugar
2 t. salt
4 c. all-purpose flour
1 egg yolk
1 T. water
1/4 c. coarse salt

In a large bowl, dissolve yeast in very warm water,
110 degrees. Add sugar and salt; stir until dissolved.
Add flour, one cup at a time; mix well. Turn dough
out onto a floured surface; knead for 5 minutes.
Divide dough into 2 parts; divide each half into 8
pieces. Roll into thin ropes; shape into pretzel twists.
Place pretzels on well-greased baking sheets.
Whisk together egg yolk and water in a cup; brush
over tops of pretzels and sprinkle with salt. Bake at
425 degrees for 15 to 20 minutes, until golden.

Makes 16 pretzels.

BACON-STUFFED MUSHROOMS

**DALE DRIGGERS
LEXINGTON, SC**

*These yummy tidbits disappear the minute I put them on the table.
A requested dish everywhere I go!*

8-oz. pkg. cream cheese,
  softened
1/2 lb. bacon, crisply
  cooked and crumbled
1/4 t. garlic powder
2 lbs. whole button
  mushrooms, stems
  removed

In a bowl, mix together cream cheese, bacon and
garlic powder until well blended. Spoon mixture into
mushroom caps; place on a baking sheet sprayed
with non-stick vegetable spray. Bake at 400 degrees
for 15 to 20 minutes, until lightly golden and heated
through. Serve warm.

Makes 12 servings.

CHICKEN RANCH DIP

NANCY LANNING
LANCASTER, SC

Recently I made this dip for a Christmas party, adding cranberries and pecans to a recipe I already had. It was definitely a hit! Some dipper ideas...crackers, pretzels, carrot and celery sticks. The dip is pretty thick, so make sure your dippers are sturdy!

Combine all ingredients together in a large bowl; blend well. Cover and refrigerate until serving time.

Makes 20 servings.

- 2 8-oz. pkg's. cream cheese, room temperature
- 12-1/2 oz. can chicken, drained and flaked
- 1 c. shredded Cheddar cheese
- 1-oz. pkg. ranch salad dressing mix
- 1 c. sweetened dried cranberries
- 1 c. chopped pecans

SO-GOOD GUACAMOLE

VICKIE
GOOSEBERRY PATCH

This guac recipe is always the first bowl to be empty at potlucks. It's almost foolproof and oh-so-good!

Scoop pulp out of avocados into a bowl. Mash to desired consistency with a potato masher. Add remaining ingredients; mix well. Serve with your favorite tortilla chips.

Makes 2 cups.

- 4 avocados, halved and pitted
- 1 onion, chopped
- 2 cloves garlic, minced
- 2 T. lime juice
- 1/8 t. kosher salt
- tortilla chips

CHAPTER SIX

DANCE THE CHARLESTON

Desserts

THERE IS ALWAYS ROOM FOR DESSERT. SO WHEN YOUR SWEET TOOTH IS CALLING, THESE SIMPLE SWEETS ARE THE PERFECT WAY TO END THE DAY.

UPSIDE-DOWN
APPLE-PECAN PIE

FRANCINE BRYSON
PICKENS, SC

Both my grandmothers used to make this pie. Over the years, I tweaked it and even won the North Carolina State Apple Cook-Off Grand Champion with it!

1/2 c. butter, softened

1-1/2 c. pecan halves

1-1/2 c. brown sugar, packed

2 9-inch pie crusts, unbaked

1/2 c. sugar

2 T. lemon juice

1 t. vanilla extract

3 T. all-purpose our

1 T. apple pie spice

1-1/8 t. cinnamon

1/2 t. nutmeg

3 c. Honey Crisp apples, peeled, cored and sliced

3 c. Swiss Gourmet apples, peeled, cored and sliced

Spread butter in the bottom and up the sides of a 9" deep-dish pie plate. Arrange pecans over butter, flat-side up, to cover pie plate. Sprinkle brown sugar over pecans. Place one crust on top; press into pie plate. In a large bowl, combine sugar, lemon juice, vanilla, flour and spices; mix well. Add apples; toss until coated. Spoon apple mixture evenly into crust. Add remaining crust. Fold over edges and crimp together; pierce several times with a fork. Bake at 450 degrees for 10 minutes. Reduce heat to 350 degrees; bake for another 45 minutes. Remove from oven; let stand until bubbling stops. While pie is still hot, invert a plate over pie and flip pie over onto plate. Pecans are now on top. Serve warm.

Serves 8.

IRISH LACE COOKIES

LAURIE RUPSIS
AIKEN, SC

These cookies are very delicate but well worth baking! They do not freeze well, but are quick & easy to do the day you need them.

In a large bowl, blend butter and brown sugar until fluffy. Beat in flour, milk and vanilla; stir in oats. Drop dough by rounded teaspoonfuls onto aluminum foil-lined baking sheets, no more than 12 per sheet. Bake at 350 degrees for 10 to 12 minutes, until golden. Allow cookies to cool on baking sheets for one minutes. Carefully remove to wire racks to cool completely.

Makes 3 dozen.

- 1/2 c. butter, softened
- 3/4 c. light brown sugar, packed
- 2 T. all-purpose flour
- 2 T. milk
- 1 t. vanilla extract
- 1-1/2 c. long-cooking oats, uncooked

MARTHA'S BROWNIE BARS

TERESA JORDAN
EASLEY, SC

This recipe for brown sugar brownies was given to my grandmother by her friend, Martha. Our whole family loves them. They are so yummy... it's hard to eat just one!

Place butter in a 13"x9" baking pan. Set in a 350-degree oven to melt; let cool slightly. Place brown sugar in a bowl; pour melted butter over brown sugar. Add eggs, vanilla, flour and nuts, if using; mix well and pour back into same baking pan. Bake at 350 degrees for 10 minutes. Reduce oven temperature to 325 degrees; bake for an additional 25 to 30 minutes. Cool completely; slice into bars. Top with whipped topping, if desired.

Makes 1-1/2 to 2 dozen.

- 3/4 c. butter
- 2 c. brown sugar, packed
- 3 eggs, beaten
- 1 t. vanilla extract
- 2 c. self-rising flour
- Optional: 1 c. chopped pecans
- Optional: whipped topping

SLUDGE PUDDING

BETHANNA KORTIE
GREER, SC

My mom used to make Fudge Batter Pudding when I was growing up and it was one of my favorites. A few years ago I asked her for the recipe so that my family could enjoy it, too. One day, my daughter made it for company. I was horrified when I saw the results...it was pitch-black! Then I realized she'd used dark chocolate cocoa, not regular baking cocoa. Our guests said the pudding looked like motor oil, but tasted delicious! We have now dubbed it "Sludge Pudding."

2 T. butter, melted
1 c. sugar, divided
1 t. vanilla extract
1 c. all-purpose flour
1 t. baking powder
3/4 t. salt, divided
8 T. dark chocolate
  baking cocoa, divided
1/2 c. milk
1-2/3 c. boiling water
Garnish: vanilla ice
  cream

In a large bowl, blend together butter, 1/2 cup sugar and vanilla; set aside. In a separate bowl, sift together flour, baking powder, 1/2 teaspoon salt and 3 tablespoons cocoa. Add flour mixture to butter mixture alternately with milk; stir well and set aside. In another bowl, combine boiling water and remaining sugar, cocoa and salt; spoon mixture into a greased 10"x6" baking pan. Drop batter over hot cocoa mixture by tablespoonfuls. Bake, uncovered, at 350 degrees for 40 to 45 minutes. Serve warm, topped with a scoop of ice cream.

Makes 6 servings.

CRANBERRY COOKIES

GLENDA TOLBERT
MOORE, SC

I fell in love with this cookie when I first encountered it at a church tea party. No detail was spared...a historic home was rented, everyone brought their own tea cups and favorite cookies. The only oversight...the hostesses forgot to boil water for our tea! It didn't take long before the situation was remedied and we were sampling different flavors of tea. Since then, I serve this cookie at the holidays. My relatives insist on it!

In a large bowl, blend butter and sugars. Add eggs, vanilla and orange oil; mix well. In a separate bowl, mix flour, baking soda and salt; add to butter mixture and stir well. Fold in remaining ingredients. Drop dough by rounded tablespoonfuls onto greased baking sheets. Bake at 350 degrees for 15 minutes, until edges are golden; check at 12 minutes. Cool on wire rack.

Makes about 3 dozen.

1 c. butter, softened
1 c. brown sugar, packed
1/3 c. sugar
2 eggs, beaten
1 t. vanilla extract
2 t. orange flavoring oil
1-1/2 c. all-purpose flour
1 t. baking soda
1/2 t. salt
3 c. quick-cooking oats, uncooked
1 c. white chocolate chips
1 c. chopped walnuts
6-oz. pkg. sweetened dried cranberries

COCONUT-CREAM CHEESE POUND CAKE

LAURIE RUPSIS
AIKEN, SC

I got this recipe from a friend ages ago! It has become a favorite at our church and is a go-to dessert for the bereavement committee when we host after-funeral receptions. But it's much too delicious not to enjoy on happier occasions as well.

1/2 c. butter, room temperature

1/2 c. butter-flavored shortening, room temperature

8-oz. pkg. cream cheese, room temperature

3 c. sugar

6 eggs

1 t. coconut flavoring

1 t. vanilla extract

3 c. all-purpose flour

1/4 t. baking soda

1/4 t. salt

6-oz. pkg. frozen flaked coconut, thawed

In a large bowl, blend together butter, shortening and cream cheese; gradually stir in sugar. Beat in eggs, one at a time; add flavorings. In a separate bowl, combine flour, baking soda and salt. Add flour mixture to butter mixture; stir just until blended. Fold in coconut. Pour batter into a greased 10" tube pan or 2 greased 9"x5" loaf pans. Bake at 325 degrees for 1-1/2 hours. Cool in pan 15 minutes before removing from pan. This cake freezes very well.

Makes 20 servings.

DINNERTIME CONVERSATION

The indigo plant is significant to South Carolina's development, as it formed a large portion of South Carolina's exports in the 1700s. The state still features frequent patches of the bright blue plants coveted for their healing powers and vibrant color.

ORANGE-PINEAPPLE CAKE

GLENDA TOLBERT
MOORE, SC

This recipe won "Best Cake" at our church. It's great for showers or just whenever you need a quick dessert.

Bake cake according to package directions, using a greased 12"x9" baking pan. Cool completely. In a separate bowl, combine whipped topping, dry pudding mix and pineapple; mix well. Thin with a little of the reserved pineapple juice, if desired. Spread over cake; garnish with oranges, if desired.

Makes 8 to 10 servings.

16-1/2 oz. pkg. orange supreme cake mix

8-oz. container frozen whipped topping, thawed

1.34-oz. pkg. sugar-free instant vanilla pudding mix

15-oz. can crushed pineapple, drained and juice reserved

Optional: mandarin oranges

BUTTERSCOTCH SPICE COOKIES

KRISTY MARKNERS
FORT MILL, SC

These are the easiest cookies to make...my two-year-old son loves them!

Combine dry cake mix, eggs, applesauce and vanilla in a large bowl. Add oats, if using. Beat with an electric mixer on low speed until well blended. Stir in butterscotch chips. Drop by rounded teaspoonfuls, 2 inches apart, on parchment paper-lined baking sheets. Bake at 375 degrees for 8 to 10 minutes, until set. Cool cookies for 2 minutes on baking sheets. Remove to wire racks to finish cooling.

Makes about 3 dozen.

18-oz. pkg. spice cake mix

2 eggs, beaten

1/2 c. applesauce

1 T. vanilla extract

Optional: 1 c. long-cooking oats, uncooked

11-oz. pkg. butterscotch chips

SOUR CREAM-CHOCOLATE CHIP CAKE

**NANCY WILSON
MURRELLS INLET, SC**

My family & friends are constantly asking me to bake this cake. It has the texture of a pound cake with the sweetness of a brownie... it's a huge hit! Baked in a tube pan, it makes a pretty presentation too.

3 c. all-purpose flour
1/4 t. baking soda
1 c. butter, softened
2 c. sugar
6 eggs
1 t. vanilla extract
8-oz. container sour cream
6-oz. pkg. mini semi-sweet chocolate chips
Optional: powdered sugar

In a bowl, stir together flour and baking soda; set aside. In a separate bowl, beat butter and sugar with an electric mixer on medium speed until fluffy. Beat in eggs, one at a time, until smooth; add vanilla. Beat in sour cream alternately with flour mixture. Fold in chocolate chips. Pour batter into a well greased and floured 10" fluted tube pan. Bake at 350 degrees for one hour and 15 minutes, or until a toothpick comes out clean. Cool; turn cake out onto a serving plate. Sprinkle with powdered sugar, if desired. Slice to serve.

Makes 12 servings.

ORANGE ICE CREAM DESSERT

**NANCY LANNING
LANCASTER, SC**

When we were young, my grandmother made this for us and we loved it! It was just like having an orange & cream frozen pop from the ice cream truck that went through our town in the evenings.

3-oz. pkg. orange gelatin mix
2 c. vanilla ice cream, softened
1 c. boiling water

In a bowl, dissolve gelatin mix in boiling water. Gradually add softened ice cream; stir with a whisk until smooth. Spoon into 4 dessert bowls. Cover and chill until set.

Serves 4.

ORANGE GINGERBREAD CUT-OUTS

ZOE BENNETT
COLUMBIA, SC

Fresh orange zest gives these gingerbread cookies an extra zing! One of my favorite cookie recipes from early fall until the end of the holiday season.

In a bowl, mix flour, baking soda, salt and ginger; set aside. In a separate large bowl, combine molasses, brown sugar, butter, egg and orange zest. Beat with an electric mixer on medium speed until smooth and creamy. Add flour mixture; beat on low speed until well mixed. Divide dough into 2 balls. Cover and refrigerate one to 2 hours, until firm. Using one ball of dough at a time, roll out 1/4-inch thick on a well-floured surface. Cut out with desired cookie cutters. Place on greased baking sheets, one inch apart. Bake at 375 degrees for 6 to 8 minutes, until cookies spring back when touched. Cool completely on wire racks. Decorate cookies as desired with Powdered Sugar Frosting, colored sugar and candies.

Makes about 4 dozen.

Powdered Sugar Frosting:
Combine powdered sugar, butter and vanilla in a large bowl. Beat with an electric mixer on low speed, adding milk to desired consistency. Tint frosting with food coloring, if desired.

2-3/4 c. all-purpose flour
1/2 t. baking soda
1/2 t. salt
1 t. ground ginger
2/3 c. light molasses
1/3 c. brown sugar, packed
1/3 c. butter, softened
1 egg, beaten
2 t. orange zest
Garnish: colored sugar, mini candies

POWDERED SUGAR FROSTING:
4 c. powdered sugar
1/2 c. butter, softened
2 t. vanilla extract
3 to 4 T. milk
Optional: few drops food coloring

GRANNY'S POUND CAKE

VICI RANDOLPH
GAFFNEY, SC

My granny has made this pound cake all my life. She has changed it so many times with different flavors of extract...I don't know if we ever had the same kind twice! I can remember Granny fussing at me when I was little because I would pick the crunchy topping off the pound cakes she made. It is still my favorite part of the cake today.

1/2 c. butter, softened
1/2 c. shortening
3 c. sugar
5 eggs
3 c. cake flour
1/2 t. baking powder
1 c. milk
2 t. vanilla, lemon or almond extract

Blend together butter, shortening and sugar. Add eggs, one at a time; beat well after each. In a separate bowl, sift together flour and baking powder. Add flour mixture to butter mixture, alternating with milk. Beat well; stir in extract. Pour batter into a greased 9" Bundt® pan. Place pan in a cold oven. Set to 325 degrees and bake for about 2 hours, or until a toothpick inserted in center tests clean.

Makes 20 to 25 servings.

AMAZING PEANUT BUTTER COOKIES

NANCY LANNING
LANCASTER, SC

Since our daughter Rebekah needs to be gluten-free, we make these cookies often....we all love them. They really are amazing!

1 c. creamy peanut butter
1/2 c. brown sugar, packed
1/2 c. sugar
1 egg, beaten
1 t. baking soda
Optional: 1/2 c. semi-sweet chocolate chips
Garnish: sugar

In a bowl, mix all ingredients except garnish. Form dough into balls by tablespoonfuls; roll balls in sugar. Place on a parchment paper-lined baking sheet; do not press down. Bake at 350 degrees for 10 to 12 minutes. Let cool on baking sheet; remove to a wire rack.

Makes 15.

CAKE MIX COOKIES

**KAREN HUGHES
NEWBERRY, SC**

This recipe is so simple and fun so everyone in the family can get involved. We have a lot of fun creating new batches. Just go by the basic recipe and then make cookies for any & all occasions. We have been labeled the best cookie makers in our area. Enjoy!

In a large bowl, beat together dry cake mix, eggs, water and oil. Fold in choice of candy, nuts or fruit. Drop dough by teaspoonfuls onto ungreased baking sheets. Bake at 350 degrees for 9 to 11 minutes.

Makes 3 dozen.

Flavor variations:

- White cake mix with chopped coconut-almond candy bars
- Yellow cake mix with candy-coated chocolates
- Chocolate cake mix with butterscotch chips or candy corn
- Carrot cake mix with raisins and chopped pecans
- Butter pecan cake mix with chopped pecan cookies
- Red velvet cake mix with white chocolate chips

18-oz. pkg. favorite-flavor cake mix
2 eggs, beaten
2 T. water
1/2 c. oil
1 c. chopped candy, nuts or dried fruit

PUMPKIN OATMEAL SCOTCHIES

KRISTY MARKNERS
FORT MILL, SC

These are my husband's favorite cookie. This is my healthier version...our kids Kaleb and Makenzy love them!

1-1/4 c. all-purpose flour
1 t. baking soda
1/2 t. cinnamon
1/2 c. butter, softened
1/2 c. canned pumpkin
3/4 c. sugar
3/4 c. brown sugar, packed
1 T. flax seed
1 egg, beaten
3 T. water
1 t. vanilla extract
1 c. butterscotch chips
3 c. long-cooking oats, uncooked

Combine flour, baking soda and cinnamon; set aside. In a separate bowl, remaining ingredients except butterscotch chips and oats; mix well. Gradually stir in flour mixture; fold in butterscotch chips and oats. Spoon dough by heaping teaspoonfuls onto parchment paper-lined baking sheets. Bake at 375 degrees for 9 to 12 minutes, until golden.

Makes 4 dozen.

DINNERTIME CONVERSATION

Summerville, is the birthplace of sweet tea. They have a "Sweet Tea Trail" that guides you through all things sweet tea and southern hospitality.

KAREN'S FRENCH APPLE PIE

KAREN CROSBY
MYRTLE BEACH, SC

I have been making this pie with its sweet, crunchy topping for as long as I can remember. I first started making it for my grandmother. It was her favorite...I was so proud! Now I'm always asked to bring it to family gatherings.

Spoon pie filling into pie crust. Combine together flour, brown sugar and butter until crumbly. Sprinkle over pie filling. Sprinkle with cinnamon to taste. Bake at 400 degrees for 30 minutes, until golden.

Serves 8.

21-oz. can apple pie filling
9-inch deep-dish pie crust, unbaked
1 c. all-purpose flour
1 c. brown sugar, packed
1/2 c. butter, softened
cinnamon to taste

FAVORITE CRANBERRY CRUNCH

SHARON WINTERS
ANDERSON, SC

This dessert is from a close friend and neighbor in the Chicago area. We shared Thanksgiving and Christmas every year, so when we moved south I brought along the recipe to continue the tradition.

Toss apples, cranberries and sugar together; put into a lightly greased 13"x9" baking pan. Mix together remaining ingredients except butter; pour over apple mixture. Drizzle with butter. Bake at 350 degrees for 45 minutes.

Makes 8 to 10 servings.

3 c. McIntosh apples, cored and coarsely chopped
2 c. cranberries
3/4 c. sugar
1-1/2 c. long-cooking oats, uncooked
3/4 c. chopped pecans
1/2 c. light brown sugar, packed
1/3 c. all-purpose flour
1/2 c. butter, melted

CHERI'S RED VELVET CAKE

**CHERI CROCKER
ANDERSON, SC**

This very moist cake is great for Christmas!

**18-1/4 oz. pkg. red velvet
cake mix**

2 c. walnuts, crushed

**18-1/4 oz. pkg. milk
chocolate cake mix**

FLUFFY FROSTING:

**2 8-oz. pkgs. cream
cheese, softened**

**2 16-oz. pkgs. powdered
sugar**

1 c. margarine, softened

2 t. vanilla extract

2 to 4 t. milk

In separate bowls, prepare cake batters according to package directions. Combine both batters in a large bowl; mix well. Pour into 2, greased and floured 13"x9" baking pans. Bake at 350 degrees for 30 to 40 minutes, until a toothpick inserted near the center comes out clean. Let cakes cool for one hour; turn out of pans onto serving plates. Prepare Fluffy Icing and spread over sides and tops of cakes; sprinkle with walnuts.

Makes 2 cakes, each serving 10 to 12.

Fluffy Frosting:
In a large bowl, combine cream cheese and powdered sugar. Beat with an electric mixer set on medium speed. Add margarine and vanilla; blend well. Add milk, a teaspoon at a time, until desired consistency is achieved.

FANTASTIC PEANUT BUTTER FUDGE

NANCY KAISER
YORK, SC

Everybody's favorite fudge! I have made this every Thanksgiving and Christmas for the last 50 years...I started very young! My mother-in-law gave me this recipe when we first got married. My father-in law probably wouldn't care if we had anything else to eat, as long as we had this fudge. I make sure that he gets it for every holiday.

In a heavy kettle over medium heat, combine butter, evaporated milk and sugar. Cook, stirring constantly, until mixture comes to the soft-ball stage, or 234 to 243 degrees on a candy thermometer. Remove from heat. Add remaining ingredients; mix well, but do not scrape sides of pan. Pour into a buttered 15"x10" jelly-roll pan. Let stand until set; cut into squares.

Makes about 4 pounds.

1 c. butter

12-oz. can evaporated milk

4 c. sugar

7-oz. jar marshmallow creme

1-3/4 c. creamy peanut butter

2 c. chopped peanuts or walnuts

PEACHY FRUIT SORBET

ZOE BENNETT
COLUMBIA, SC

So refreshing! Garnish with fruit slices.

Place fruit on a wax paper-lined baking sheet. Cover and freeze for about 2 hours, until completely frozen. Combine fruit, water and lemon juice in a food processor; process until smooth. Serve immediately, or spoon into a covered container and freeze up to 2 weeks.

Makes 4 servings.

1 peach, peeled, pitted and cubed

1 c. mango, peeled, pitted and cubed

1 ripe banana, peeled and mashed

2 T. water

1 T. lemon juice

MATTIE LOU'S PRUNE CAKE

BETTY SANDERS
TOWNVILLE, SC

This recipe was handed down from my grandmother, Mattie Lou, who would only make it during the Christmas holiday. It has been a tradition each Christmas and is a special request at Thanksgiving by my son, Brian, and husband, Keith.

2 c. sugar
2 c. self-rising flour
1 T. pumpkin pie spice
3 eggs, beaten
1 c. oil
4 2-1/2 oz. jars prune baby food
1 t. vanilla extract
Optional: 3/4 c. chopped pecans

Mix sugar, flour and spice together in a large bowl. Blend in eggs, oil, prunes and vanilla; mix thoroughly. Stir in pecans, if desired. Pour batter into a greased and floured tube pan. Bake at 350 degrees for approximately one hour, until a toothpick inserted in center comes out clean. Let cool on wire rack.

Makes 12 to 14 servings.

GIVE-ME-THAT-RECIPE POUND CAKE

GLENDA TOLBERT
MOORE, SC

This recipe was handed down from my great-grandmother and grandmother, and is served at all family gatherings. When I take it to church I'm always asked for the recipe. For a divine dessert, garnish with sliced strawberries or peaches and whipped cream.

1 c. shortening
2-1/2 c. sugar
5 eggs
1 t. lemon flavoring
3 c. all-purpose flour
1 t. baking powder
1 c. milk

In a large bowl, beat shortening and sugar for 2 minutes. Add eggs, one at a time; add flavoring and set aside. In a separate bowl, mix together flour and baking powder; add to shortening mixture alternately with milk, mixing until just combined. Pour batter into a greased and floured Bundt® pan. Bake at 350 degrees for about one hour, until a toothpick inserted near the center tests clean. Cool in pan; turn out and cool completely before slicing.

Makes 16 servings.

SOUR CREAM COOKIES

NANCY KAISER
YORK, SC

This was my husband's grandmother's recipe. My father-in-law said that whenever he and his brothers came in from school or from doing their farm chores, his mother always had a jar full of these big, thick, soft and delicious cookies waiting for them. I've revised it somewhat and added the amounts of a few ingredients. I like to use a scalloped round cookie cutter.

In a large bowl, blend together shortening, sour cream, brown sugar and egg; set aside. In a separate bowl, combine flour, baking soda and nutmeg; mix well and add to shortening mixture. Mix until well blended. Cover and chill for 2 hours, or overnight. On a floured surface, roll out dough about 1/2-inch thick. Cut out with a 3" round cookie cutter; arrange cookies on ungreased baking sheets. Bake at 375 degrees for 13 to 14 minutes.

Makes 2-1/2 dozen.

1 c. butter-flavored or regular shortening

8-oz. container sour cream

2-1/2 c. brown sugar, packed

1 egg, beaten

5-1/2 c. all-purpose flour

1 t. baking soda

1 t. nutmeg

CARAMEL MARSHMALLOWS

NANCY LANNING
LANCASTER, SC

When we were in Iowa for a few years, these were a favorite with all the kids...easy for kids to make too!

Combine caramels, condensed milk and butter in a large saucepan over low heat. Cook and stir until melted. Using a long toothpick, dip each marshmallow in mixture; roll in cereal. Place on wax paper to set. Store in a covered container.

Makes about 4 dozen.

40 caramels, unwrapped

1/2 c. sweetened condensed milk

1/2 c. butter

50 marshmallows

6 c. crispy rice cereal

MINTY CHOCOLATE BROWNIES

KRISTY MARKNERS
FORT MILL, SC

These brownies feature my five-year-old son's favorite cookie...and any brownie that has crushed cookies as one of its ingredients has got to be good!

1/2 c. butter, melted
1 c. sugar
1 t. vanilla extract
2 eggs
1/2 c. all-purpose flour
1/3 c. baking cocoa
1/4 t. baking powder
1/4 t. salt
1/4 c. milk
7 chocolate-covered thin mint cookies, crushed

In a bowl, beat together butter, sugar and vanilla with an electric mixer on medium speed. Beat in eggs, one at a time, until fully combined. In a separate bowl, stir together flour, cocoa, baking powder and salt. Slowly add flour mixture to butter mixture, beating until well blended. Beat in milk. Fold in crushed cookies. Spread batter evenly in a lightly greased 9"x9" baking pan. Bake at 350 degrees for 35 to 40 minutes, until a toothpick inserted near the center tests clean. Cool completely in pan on a wire rack. Cut into squares.

Makes one dozen.

SCHOOLHOUSE PEANUT BUTTER FUDGE

SONYA PLESSINGER
LORIS, SC

I got this recipe from my Aunt Mary Lee who worked in my elementary school cafeteria years ago. I make it so often I know it by memory. It's easy, with no cooking, and everybody loves it.

1/2 c. margarine, softened
3/4 c. creamy peanut butter
16-oz. pkg. powdered sugar
1 t. vanilla extract

In a bowl, stir together margarine and powdered sugar until creamy. Add peanut butter and vanilla; mix well. Press into an ungreased 9"x9" baking pan; flatten surface. Cut into small squares. Cover and store in a cool dark place. Fudge will dry out somewhat if refrigerated, but will still taste good.

Makes 4 dozen pieces.

GRANDMA SAINT'S FRIDGE COOKIES

**MARY ANN SAINT
INDIAN LAND, SC**

My sister-in-law in Louisiana always made these cookies for us when we visited. She knew my husband would be so happy to eat the cookies his mother used to make. In fact, it made all of us happy...they're the most delicious refrigerator cookies I've ever tasted. You can't eat just one...they are addictive!

In a large bowl, blend butter and sugars. Add egg and vanilla; mix well. In a separate bowl, mix together remaining ingredients except pecans. Add flour mixture to butter mixture and stir well; add pecans. Divide dough into 2 parts. Form each part into a roll; wrap rolls in wax paper. Refrigerate at least 2 hours to overnight. Cut dough into 1/2-inch thick slices; arrange 2 inches apart on lightly greased baking sheets. Bake at 350 degrees for 14 to 15 minutes.

Makes 4 dozen.

1 c. butter, softened
1/2 c. sugar
1/2 c. brown sugar, packed
1 egg, beaten
1 t. vanilla extract
2 c. all-purpose flour
1/2 t. baking soda
1/4 t. salt
1 c. chopped pecans

KITCHEN TIP

Easily make your own buttermilk by adding a tablespoon of vinegar or lemon juice to 1 cup of milk.

INDEX

INDEX continued

U.S. to METRIC RECIPE EQUIVALENTS

Volume Measurements

¼ teaspoon. . . . . 1 mL
½ teaspoon. . . . . 2 mL
1 teaspoon . . . . 5 mL
1 tablespoon = 3 teaspoons. . . . . . 15 mL
2 tablespoons = 1 fluid ounce . . . . 30 mL
¼ cup. . . . . 60 mL
⅓ cup. . . . . 75 mL
½ cup = 4 fluid ounces. . . . . 125 mL
1 cup = 8 fluid ounces . . . . 250 mL
2 cups = 1 pint = 16 fluid ounces 500 mL
4 cups = 1 quart . . . . 1 L

Weights

1 ounce . . . . 30 g
4 ounces . . . . 120 g
8 ounces . . . . 225 g
16 ounces = 1 pound . . . . 450 g

Baking Pan Sizes

Square
8x8x2 inches . . . . 2 L = 20x20x5 cm
9x9x2 inches . . . . . . 2.5 L = 23x23x5 cm

Rectangular
13x9x2 inches . . . . . 3.5 L = 33x23x5 cm

Loaf
9x5x3 inches . . . . 2 L = 23x13x7 cm

Round
8x1½ inches . . . . 1.2 L = 20x4 cm
9x1½ inches . . . . 1.5 L = 23x4 cm

Recipe Abbreviations

t. = teaspoon. . . . . ltr. = liter
T. = tablespoon. . . . . oz. = ounce
c. = cup. . . . . lb. = pound
pt. = pint. . . . . .doz. = dozen
qt. = quart. . . . . .pkg. = package
gal. = gallon. . . . . .env. = envelope

Oven Temperatures
300° F. . . . . .150° C
325° F. . . . . .160° C
350° F. . . . . .180° C
375° F. . . . . .190° C
400° F. . . . . .200° C
450° F. . . . . .230° C

Kitchen Measurements
A pinch = ⅛ tablespoon
1 fluid ounce = 2 tablespoons
3 teaspoons = 1 tablespoon
4 fluid ounces = ½ cup
2 tablespoons = ⅛ cup
8 fluid ounces = 1 cup
4 tablespoons = ¼ cup
16 fluid ounces = 1 pint
8 tablespoons = ½ cup
32 fluid ounces = 1 quart
16 tablespoons = 1 cup
16 ounces net weight = 1 pound
2 cups = 1 pint
4 cups = 1 quart
4 quarts = 1 gallon

Send us your favorite recipe

and the memory that makes it special for you!*

If we select your recipe for a brand-new **Gooseberry Patch** cookbook, your name will appear right along with it...and you'll receive a FREE copy of the book!

Submit your recipe on our website at

www.gooseberrypatch.com/sharearecipe

*Please include the number of servings and all other necessary information.

Have a taste for more?

Visit www.gooseberrypatch.com to join our Circle of Friends!

- Free recipes, tips and ideas plus a complete cookbook index
- Get mouthwatering recipes and special email offers delivered to your inbox.

You'll also love these cookbooks from **Gooseberry Patch**!

A Year Of Holidays
Christmas for Sharing
Classic Church Potlucks
Farmhouse Kitchen
Our Best Cast-Iron Cooking Recipes
Our Best Recipes from Grandma's Cookie Jar
Quick & Easy Recipes with Help
Shortcuts to Grandma's Best Recipes
Slow Cookers, Casseroles & Skillets
Welcome Autumn

www.gooseberrypatch.com